BUILT
FOR THIS

FROM TRIALS TO TRIUMPH, GUIDED BY FAITH AND LOVE

ARMANDO & PEARL NAVA

Fedd Books
P.O. Box 341973
Austin, TX 78734

www.thefeddagency.com

Published in association with The Fedd Agency, Inc., a literary agency.

ISBN: 978-1-964508-17-7

LCCN: 2024911538

Printed in the United States of America

*We dedicate this book to our incredible parents, who gave
their all and made the most of what they had.*

Table of Contents

CHAPTER 1

Armando

Early years McAllen, TX

Train up a child in the way he should go; even when he is old, he will not depart from it.

—PROVERBS 22:6

It's time to end this, I think, as my finger hovers over my computer mouse.

My heart begins to pound like a war drum while I scroll through countless videos I've posted online over the last four years of my life.

My YouTube channel, *Navathebeast*, was the first official military influencer account and garnered millions of views and subscribers. That kind of influence translated into fame on camera and a pile of cash and women off camera. At one time I enjoyed the spoils of my online empire. But like most empires, it wouldn't last. There was no foundation laid down for the hollow house I had built.

I mute the volume on my computer. I feel disgusted listening to the youthful voice behind the high-energy YouTube persona I had created.

The man on camera is the spitting image of Armando Nava. We have the same features, hair, and laugh. But we are not the same person. Not anymore.

I breathe in and close my eyes.

"You can do this," my wife says gently, and rubs my shoulder. "We can do this. God will provide."

The yellow glow of the computer bounces off her face, and I see my videos in the reflection of her glasses. An influencer shutting down their own social media account is like a baker setting fire to their own bakery. My social media accounts were more than my business, they were my entire identity.

Suddenly, I am reminded of the verse in 2 Corinthians:

> *"Therefore, if anyone is in Christ, he is a new creation. The old has passed away; behold, the new has come."*
>
> — 2 CORINTHIANS 5:17

I take one final glance at the collection of usernames and comments underneath some of my favorite videos. An ego-stroking collection that encompassed caustic to adoration.

Ok. Let's go!

Click, click, click.

"This will permanently delete your YouTube data," the pop-up screen says.

A blue box with the words "Delete my Content" is one click away.

I – KING OF ASADA

Before I was "Navathebeast," I was the second son born to Maria and Armando Nava Sr.

I was proudly raised in the Rio Grande Valley, or the RGV as locals call it.

My grandparents emigrated from Mexico to the USA at the turn of the century and made the bordertown of McAllen, Texas, our home.

Driving around McAllen back in the late 1990s and early 2000s you'd see a lot of rundown houses with equally worn-out cars left out in the front yard. No time to tend to a lawn, mend a fence, or paint a patio when parents are working two and three odd jobs at a time.

There was more dirt than driveway in my hometown, and you'd know it was Saturday by the sound of tires flying through gravel roads and car radios turned on full blast. Every weekend generations of families would pour into each other's backyards and party till the early hours of the night.

McAllen was the epitome of a work-hard-play-hard town.

Plumes of smoke would rise from each family's backyards with the tantalizing smell of *carne asada* filling the air. These *asadas* are social events and centered around a barbeque with plenty of marinated meats, salsas, and ice-cold beer. The parties could get pretty crazy, and often ended with couples hollering at each other or breaking something.

My father was the king of the *asada*.

His big personality was on display for our neighbors and family members as he worked the barbecue and handed out beer to the neighbors.

When I was five years old, I remember opening the backdoor to our yard and seeing my parents through the crowd. It was always strange to see Dad in his casual clothes. Like catching a teacher at the supermarket, it was a bit disconcerting to see him out of his work clothes of black suit, black tie, and black briefcase. Dad worked in real estate and was a salesman.

I made my way through the sea of familiar faces from the neighborhood before finding my parents over by the barbecue. My Dad had a beer in his hand. It must have been his third or fourth, because he was a touch softer with me when he drank.

"*Mijo*," he said, as he put his strong hand on my shoulder and looked me in the eyes.

I waited.

For a second, I imagined him scooping me up and saying words I'd never heard him say, "I love you son! I'm so proud of you."

"Sonny," he said again, as he furrowed his brow.

"What, Dad?" I searched his face.

"Nothing, *Mandito*!" he smiled, and went back to the barbecue.

"Mandito" is what he called me.

My Mother made her way over to us. High heels, short skirt, and perfectly styled hair; at only twenty-five years old, she was always ready to party. She looked at Dad with a grimace.

"*Mandito*, can you get us some ice from inside?" she asked.

I nodded and went inside. I knew instinctively that Mom didn't really want ice. She and Dad had been in a tumultuous relationship my entire life. They were like a book of matches and gasoline, and my older brother and I knew it was only a matter of time before they'd explode.

That night as the music faded, my parents tumbled back into the house and dove into a drunken argument.

I could hear them yelling at each other.

I'd find out the full context of their conflict years later.

Earlier, Mom had made one of her famous chili bowls for Dad and called him to eat lunch with her. Dad said he was too busy for lunch. Well, that didn't sit well with Mom. He never said no to her chili. She called his office and pretended to be a client—that's when she found out through his coworker that he had gone out to lunch. After realizing he had lied to her, she followed him home after work, and her suspicions were confirmed. He was with another woman.

Mom was heartbroken and furious. She confronted him, and he denied the affair. Mom knew he was lying but wasn't financially stable enough to leave him. From that point on, their marriage was in title only. They lived two separate lives. Mom started partying with her sister, and Dad continued drinking and hosting big *carne asada* parties.

My older brother, Brandon, and I woke up to the commotion.

"I want a divorce!" I heard my mother howl. "I can't do this anymore! You're too boring, and you're a womanizer," she yelled.

"YOU? You can't do this? I can't do this! And I don't have to do this. I'm out of here," my father roared.

We heard the door slam, and he was gone.

My brother and I raced downstairs and found my mother crying into her palms.

"Where's Dad?" I asked.

"Your Dad has to go for a little bit," Mom said flatly.

"It's 3 a.m.; where does he have to go right now," asked my brother.

Mom didn't respond.

"When is he coming back?" I begged Mom for an answer.

There was a long pause, and then finally, she said, "He's not coming back. We are getting a divorce."

My brother and I both burst into tears and pulled on my mom's arms, "No, Mom! Make him come back. Don't do this!" we pleaded.

When all three of us were out of tears, we went to bed. The home felt so empty without Dad, and it never felt full again.

II – MOM

Three years had passed since Dad left us to enjoy his single life. Mom had thrown herself into her job and into the arms of many, *many* men. I never blamed her; I can only imagine the pain she was going through. She'd lost her marriage and was trying to raise two boys all by herself.

Some of her boyfriends would stick around for months at a time. Sometimes I would be excited, thinking maybe this one will be like our new dad. One guy bought my brother and me a ton of gifts and seemed to really care for my mom—but it turned out he was already married. I remember Mom taking that breakup pretty hard.

But mostly, the men would cycle through our house like Groundhog Day. Every morning, rinse and repeat.

When I was eight years old and still living in McAllen, I woke up for school and quietly walked down the stairs to the kitchen. I opened the refrigerator. Expired milk. Leftover Jack-in-the-Box burger. And a bunch of sauces. I sauntered over to the pantry and found a half-eaten box of Cheerios. When I poured a bowl of dry cereal, I noticed a pair of unfamiliar keys on the kitchen table.

Someone had spent the night.

I peered out the window over the sink and saw a beat-up truck outside.

I heard muffled voices and coy laughter coming from my mother's bedroom. Mom was never discreet with her escapades.

The doorknob rotated and Mom's bedroom door slowly opened. Out walked a towering man with a strong jawline and a beard.

I kept my head down and ate my Cheerios.

"Hey Mr.," the man said to me.

I gave him a quick nod.

By then, I was old enough to know this guy wasn't going to be a father to me. Like many who passed through our house before, they were womanizers and only there to use my Mom.

I'd watch these men blow through, seduce her, and leave in the morning.

On one occasion, I was upstairs, when my mom called for me to come out and meet her "new guy."

"*Mandito*! Come meet Esteban," she called. I could hear in her voice that she was tipsy.

By then, I knew the drill. It was a waste of my time to meet another lame dude. There was nothing down there for me.

But I went downstairs and begrudgingly said hi. I felt gross talking to him. Like we don't need to know each other. We don't need to do this.

When he left the next morning, I decided to confront my mother.

"Mom, you're just letting these guys sleep with you," I told her outright. "And you're just... you're just giving them your all. And I don't want them in our house," I said.

That conversation didn't go smoothly.

Mom fumed. She said I had no right to judge her or her decisions, and that I had no idea what it was like to be lonely.

I slinked off to my room and disappeared into my video games.

I promised myself I'd never become the type of man who uses women.

III – ESCAPE

Fortunately, my mom was hardworking. And as hard as she went at night, she went doubly or triply hard during her workday. Like my Dad, Mom was also in real estate.

When my brother and I were little, she'd take us to work every day. She sold trailer homes, and some of my earliest memories are in her office with the one-hundred-degree sun beating down on the metallic roof. My brother and I would spend the day in that heat box playing computer games like Tetris or Kinect while Mom wheeled and dealed with clients from early morning until late at night.

She was a hardcore salesperson. She'd convince client after client that *this* trailer was the home they were looking for and that it could improve their life.

I saw from a young age how my Mom's sincerity charmed her clients into signing contracts, and eventually put a new roof over *our* head. Mom bought us a home in Corpus Christ when I was in fifth grade. It was lovely, but for me, it felt false, like a model home, like we were pretending to be a family. It was always empty.

Mom hustled, and her hours were long. To unwind, Mom would go out to the clubs or hang out with her girlfriends. And I get it. Now that I am in real estate, I know firsthand how hard it is to turn off your brain after a long day.

Because mom worked so hard, most days after middle school, while my brother was with his friends, I was by myself at the house.

I would retreat into my "secret" room. It wasn't really a secret. It was a utility closet where I set up my computer on a little plastic desk.

During the school day, I counted down every hour and every minute of the bus ride until the second I could be back in my secret room and escape into my video games. It was my sanctuary. I'd lock myself in the room for hours. And on the weekend, I was there from Saturday morning at 6 a.m. to 12 midnight on Sunday.

My username was *pitplayer12*, and I had the beefiest avatar, with the physique of a 1980s Arnold Schwarzenegger. I was probably eleven or twelve years old, and I was glued to multiplayer online games like RuneScape and Call of Duty. Because I was playing online so much, I had advanced to level 99 in a lot of my specialties and one of the more feared in RuneScape. I was a ruthless player. I had an outfit called Dragon Armor that made my avatar look indestructible. Other players in the game respected me.

I pretended to be a few years older too. I had friends who I talked with everyday online, and even a sixteen-year-old girlfriend named "Skylar" who was from England. We'd go on "dates" in RuneScape where we would chop wood.

When my virtual girlfriend asked to see a picture of me, I took a black and white photo in a pair of my Dad's old Oakley sunglasses. I made sure to keep the photo vague, so I could keep the ruse up and she wouldn't know my real age. It worked.

I felt so cool when I was in that gaming world. I had so many friends online, a girlfriend, respect—but outside of the games, I had nothing. No friends, no girlfriend, and I didn't like myself.

I was so envious when my online friends would say they had to go eat dinner with their family. I'd try to keep them online for as long as I could. No one was waiting for me to eat dinner with them. Eventually, I'd lie and write something like, "Cool, man, have a good dinner. I'm going to hit the gym." I never went to the gym. I'd lock myself in the room and log in to another game.

The teens on the other side of the screen had no idea they were talking with an eleven-year-old pudgy boy who was stuffed in a smelly utility closet.

I felt powerful in the game, and figured out how I could stay there around the clock.

I used Mom's credit card to buy "bots." These robots would "work" for me all night long, so I could game even while I was asleep. A kid playing a couple of hours of RuneScape after school couldn't hold a candle to my bot empire.

And the more "loot" I'd buy, the more I'd want. So instead of playing fairly, I convinced my brother and uncle to ambush other players with me. I'd lure innocent players into my world under the guise of good intentions. Then, I'd coordinate an attack with my brother and uncle to kill the player and steal their money and armor.

Eventually, my gameplay caught up to me. I guess I "killed" the wrong guy, because I wound up in a revenge plot. A horde of one hundred bounty hunters came after me, killed me in an instant, and I lost all my money and work.

This drama felt so real to me. I felt like the stakes were high, and although what you buy in a video game is only made out of pixels, I was spending real cash to invest in my status. So, that loss was devastating. Plus, I had managed to parlay my gaming skills off the screen and into the classroom. If a classmate was familiar with my "work" inside RuneScape, I could negotiate with them. I'd trade homework assignments for loot in the video game.

While I'd game, I'd suck down a bright red Mountain Dew and an entire bag of Ruffles sour cream and onion chips. When I was done with my garbage dinner, I'd slip downstairs and take out a whole sleeve of cookie dough. I'd look at the dough and hear the last thing Mom said to me: "Don't eat the cookie dough; I'm going to bake cookies."

But she never had time to bake cookies. So, I'd eat the whole roll of dough, and then go back up to the gaming closet.

Eventually, Mom would tap on my door after her long workday. And she'd hand me a takeout bag from Jack in the Box. My order was always a large milkshake, a double-double meat burger, and curly fries. I wouldn't even get up from my seat. I'd thank her and keep playing through the night.

It got to the point where I wouldn't even shower, because I was playing nonstop. I would lock myself in my room and just play video games all day and keep eating. By middle school, I was already pushing 200 pounds.

Mom didn't have time for groceries, so when we had an opportunity to eat together as a family, we'd hightail it to the Golden Corral buffet and load up our plates until they were overflowing.

Both my brother and I began gaining weight at a rapid rate on our takeout diet.

And the more obese I became, the less time I wanted to spend at school.

School was brutal. I didn't pay attention, and I was exhausted from playing video games all night. I would call my Mom in the middle of the day pretending to be sick, just so I wouldn't have to endure another day of teasing in the classroom.

One day, in seventh grade, I was sitting at the back of a classroom in my English class when my pencil tip broke.

I sighed.

I had to make the long walk all the way from the back to the front of the classroom to sharpen my pencil. It felt like one hundred miles away. I wanted to just disappear into the walls. I squeezed through the rows of desks, slowly making my way to the front of the class.

At that point, it had been nearly thirty days since my last full-body shower. I know. I know. It's hard to believe.

As I passed by a classmate named Krista, who was wearing overalls and her hair in braids, she recoiled in her seat and shouted, "Dude, you smell like poop. You need to take a shower."

The class erupted in laughter, and my heart sank. I wanted to run back to my secret game room, shut the door, and throw away the key.

That night, I took the longest shower of my life, and when I dried off, I looked at my body in the mirror. *What happened?* I thought. How did I get like this?

I was only eleven years old and weighed more than many adult men. I found a pair of scissors and grabbed the fat around my belly. I thought, *What if I just cut all this off? Then, would I look better? Would people be my friends?* Thankfully, I didn't go through with the plan, but I realized I needed to change, and fast.

By eighth grade, I had come up with what I thought was a genius plan to lose weight. I'd skip all of my meals, and only eat a little bit of peanut butter and one apple. I'd go as many days as I could on no food, and then when I was hungry, I would eat everything in sight. I mean, I would go to town on burgers and fries and everything! And my secret to weight loss was throwing up what I had just eaten.

When I'd look in the mirror, I'd see that overweight kid in the classroom and hear my classmates laughing. So, I'd push myself to throw up whatever was in my stomach. My whole mindset was fixated on being skinny. Food had been a comfort or a sedative, but from that point on, it was something I took power over.

In a world where I felt powerless, it felt good to control something in my life. I could control the food that went into my body, and I could see my body changing. I started losing weight, but my mental health was in the toilet. Little did I know that my behavior has a clinical term: disordered eating.

IV – DONUTS AND DADS

I was always jealous of the school kids whose parents showed up to school events.

One year at school there was a "Donuts and Dads" day. Students could bring their dads to the cafeteria and enjoy some tasty Krispy Kreme donuts together.

The fathers came to our classroom to pick up their kids. One by one, my classmates happily greeted their fathers at the door and went on to get their donuts.

Soon, the only kids left in the class were me and this guy named Michael.

I turned to Michael, and said, "Looks like your dad isn't coming either?"

"Oh, no," said Michael. "He's just running late."

"Oh," my heart sank.

A few minutes later, Michael's father showed up, and he jumped up from his desk to greet him.

I put my head down on the desk and decided I'd use the time to take a nap.

Thankfully, my buddy Leo, high on sugar, raced back to the classroom and asked me if I wanted to have donuts with his dad.

"Yes!" I nearly leaped out of my seat.

I was so desperate for a role model and was the kind of kid who would have benefited from a strong father figure.

I came home and took out all my resentment on my mother. I had learned how to curse like a master and felt like if my Mom wasn't going to respect herself—by letting these dudes run all over her—then I wasn't going to respect her either.

I still found solace in my gaming closet. While other kids were sleeping, I'd game until the wee hours of the morning and sometimes find myself drifting online to pornography. I was too young to even understand what sex meant, but I was mentally downloading image after image. I'd take in videos of a dominant man who could get a woman to do whatever he wanted, and I was mesmerized. Some of the stuff I'd watch was brutal—and would involve a man physically hurting a woman. That's where my wires started to cross. Sex = brutality. Love = pain and control.

And as I grew up, eventually, I'd trade my video game console for my phone— to pursue women the same way I had seen men pursue them in pornography.

By the time puberty hit, my childhood rejections and disappointment began to manifest as anger. I was so fed up with all the men who would cycle through our home.

Often, they would try to tell me what to do or try to get me to mind them.

That kind of thing pissed me off. I remember telling this guy, "Hey, you're not the first man in this home, and you're not going to be the last. I've seen guys like you come in and out. You are just another statistic," I said calmly.

Well, he didn't like that.

He started cussing me out, and soon my mom came out of her bedroom shouting. Then the man directed his anger toward her and called her every color under the sun. My mom begged me to tell the man I was lying. I did.

This was the pattern for so many years. And our arguments had become part of our routine.

When Mom was too overwhelmed with my brother and me, she'd ship us off to our grandparents' ranch.

"Not the ranch!" we'd squeal.

The ranch was off the grid and filled with chickens, horses, and dogs. I couldn't play video games or talk to my RuneScape girlfriend out in the desert. It was terrible.

My Grandfather was a huge man who would brag about surviving a stabbing in a bar fight. He was an aggressive man and had a traditional marriage to my Grandma, who was always in the kitchen.

Ironically, while I was delighted to digitally chop trees in RuneScape, when Grandpa asked me to chop real trees on the ranch, I was absolutely miserable. I was overweight, and my Grandpa would tease both me and my brother for being chubby. Hot, humid Texas air, no internet, and getting an earful from our Grandfather. Yeah, Mom totally knew she was punishing us.

And to add insult to injury, my Grandma would put us on an extra health kick of vegetables and lentils whenever we stayed on the ranch.

My mom's younger brother, Carlos, lived at the ranch too and worked at a pizza joint.

Uncle Carlos would bring home pizzas after his shifts. In the middle of the night, I would sneak into the kitchen and go wild on the pizza. My hunger was insatiable. I ate until my stomach hurt, and then sneaked back upstairs to bed.

Uncle Carlos would be so angry when he'd find an empty pizza box and crust on the kitchen table.

"This was supposed to feed the entire family!" he'd shout.

We'd continue like this until Mom picked us up. For a few days, we were all nice to each other, and then we'd start arguing again.

One day, I was arguing with my mom in the car and she said, "I can't do this anymore."

My brother and I looked at each other in the backseat.

"What are you talking about, Mom?" my brother asked.

"I can't take care of you guys anymore. You both are like your father. So, I want you to pack your bags tonight. You can move in with your dad," she said.

And overnight, we did just that. We were back in McAllen with my father.

I was excited to be living with this man I had built up in my mind.

I remember my mom yelling at my father over the phone, ordering him to come visit us on the weekends. It was humiliating. But then Dad would pick us up from school in his gorgeous red Jaguar convertible, and we'd feel like a million bucks.

So, I was hopeful. Maybe we'd actually be buds.

Unfortunately, we moved in right when the housing market crashed. My father had lost a lot of his business and was surviving on food stamps.

Dad wasn't used to having young kids around.

One of the first nights we spent with him, I remember him tucking us into bed. He lay next to us with a TV on and pretended like he was falling asleep.

A few hours later, I woke up, and he was gone.

I was freaking out, thinking, *Where the heck did he go?* I had a flip phone and called him non-stop. He didn't answer. So, I sat up at the dining room table, waiting for him. I wound up falling asleep at the table.

When I woke up, around 7 a.m., I saw Dad passed out on the couch. He had gone out with his buddies. I smelled tacos. He brought us home some food. But I felt sick to my stomach; this was no different than my Mom's place. *I'm going to get placated with food here, too,* I thought.

For the remainder of my time living under Dad's roof, we had little to no conversation, and I started looking for role models in all the wrong places.

V – SELLING LIKE MOM AND DAD

While I floundered in school, skating by on bare minimum grades, I realized early on that I had a knack at sales.

I was still focused on losing weight but also wanted new video games. While my classmates were getting some of their first jobs at the mall or serving food, I came up with a scheme I learned through YouTube.

I asked Uncle Carlos to front me some cash so I could start my first e-commerce business.

I knew my market. All the fourteen-year-olds in McAllen were super into these "boobie bracelets" that were for breast cancer, and selfie sticks. We ordered the items in bulk and bought packaging to make our products look snazzy. I hired my brother, and the two of us went out door to door, our backpacks stuffed with merchandise.

I would talk to neighbor kids and imitate the way my mom spoke to her clients when trying to sell a house.

I'd say things like, *"Dude, this is the hottest thing ever."* I would sell them real hard. *Listen, you can go down the road but you're gonna end up paying, like, twenty bucks for the same thing, but I can give it to you for ten. But it's for a limited time only because I only have so many in my backpack. Check it out."*

We were hustlers, and with the extra cash, I was able to feed my video game addiction. I was even able to buy an Xbox.

I was making more money out of my backpack in a day than most kids would make in a week at Sonic or Whataburger!

I was still obsessed with losing weight, but I was also becoming obsessed with getting a girlfriend. I realized it was going to take more than skinny bones to attract a girl. I needed muscle. I found a guy named Shaun T and started doing a fitness program called "Insanity."

That's when I discovered weight training. I quickly realized starving myself was counterproductive to gaining muscle. I needed food to use as fuel. As I started training, I thought, *Heck since I am on this weight loss muscle-building journey, I should post my results online. Then I can sell fitness programs. I'd be the perfect testimony.*

If you don't have good leaders in front of you, you're going to look elsewhere. I had learned how to make money. But I didn't know how to be a man, how to ask a girl out. So where do you think I went for advice? YouTube.

All my heroes were online. Some of them were decent people, but mostly, the internet is a dangerous place for a young boy to learn how to be a man.

CHAPTER 2

Pearl

Sibanicú, Cuba - Houston, Texas

Before I formed you in the womb I knew you,
and before you were born, I consecrated you; I
appointed you a prophet to the nations.

—JEREMIAH 1:5

I crawled on my hands and knees from the living room into my bedroom closet. I pushed the door shut and erupted into a coughing fit from the smoke. The flames looked angry, and their appetite was insatiable. They scarfed up my curtains, dresser drawers, my passport, letters, photographs—collateral damage. All my belongings were swallowed up in the fire.

I cracked the door and, with wide eyes, watched the furious blaze envelop my bed.

Good. I thought.

The flames raced up the walls and across the ceiling. I heard a loud *pop pop pop* as the windows cracked and busted. I couldn't see as everything was filled with an inky dark smoke.

Moments ago, this was one small flame. I had taken a lighter in my hand and flicked it on and off, watching the small blue and orange flame. *Click, click, click.*

I shuddered as I stood over my bed and felt repulsed.

He would never take me on that bed again! He would never mess with me. I was done. I was done with it all. Never again.

I lit the bed on fire and watched it burn.

I intended to die that day, but praise God, He had a better plan for my life.

I – *SIBANICÚ*

Before my father was murdered, he told my pregnant mother to name me Perla.

My full name is Perla Vivianis Michel Fernandez, and my Grandparents always called me Vivianis.

I grew up in the small town of Sibanicú, in central Cuba. The population of the town rarely tips over 30,000.

To this day, Cuba is a time machine back to a simpler era. Clocks seem to run slower, and no one is in a hurry.

In Cuba, everyone looks after each other, so kids run together safe and free, like friendly wolf packs.

I was an only child, but the neighborhood was full of children, so I was never really alone. I was mostly a happy child, always smiling and laughing.

Some of my earliest memories are of dancing in the rain barefooted and carefree. It rained a lot, and whenever the clouds gathered, and the smell of rain was in the air, I would throw on my swimsuit and run outside to play in the puddles.

It was one of those long rainy afternoons when Grandmother called me inside.

I skipped inside and greeted my grandmother with three kisses.

I checked on my *cernicalo*—the small hawk lived in a room meant to be a bathroom. It squawked and fluttered around the room. Before the *cernicalo*, I had a green and yellow parrot.

My grandparents' house had two large bedrooms, but like many homes in the region, we didn't have indoor plumbing. Actually, we didn't have outdoor plumbing either! When we needed to go to the bathroom, we would go to our next-door neighbor's backyard and use their outdoor bathroom. It was a little hole in the ground. The neighbors didn't only have a better bathroom situation, they also had huge cherry trees and a massive backyard. I'd spend hours in their backyard in my own imaginary adventures.

I often pretended I was Cinderella. She was my favorite Disney princess. Looking back, I guess we had a lot in common. Cinderella grew up without her parents, was poor, and loved animals, just like me! She also had an evil stepparent, but we'll get to that part of my story later.

"Help me with this, *Vivianis*," Grandmother instructed. We ventured outside to the backyard where we drew water from a large bucket. We didn't have running water, so we'd collect rainwater for cooking and cleaning.

The day when our family finally had enough money to buy an electric water gadget was big news! You'd put the electric device in a bucket of water, and it would heat the water in an instant. Having a warm bucket bath was such a treat.

After helping Grandmother bring in the water, she started preparing dinner: rice, beans, and chicken.

I was relieved to see she had prepared chicken and not one of our pigs. I always fell in love with the pigs and had a hard time when we had to eat them.

Grandmother carefully dished out our plates. Even to this day, the Cuban government distributes portions of food to every citizen based on the size of a household. So, we'd go to the municipal food depot and receive four portions for my grandparents, my uncle, and myself.

There wasn't a ton of variety in our food rations. Bread, beans, and local fruits like mangos and starfruit. As a child, I thought that the only food that existed in the world was what was given out at the depot. In fact, I had only seen exotic fruits like pears, blueberries, and strawberries in a still-life painting that hung on my neighbor's wall. It might as well have been a painting of a unicorn. When I looked at the painting, I thought it was drawn from some-one's imagination, as I didn't believe such foods existed in the world.

After dinner I cozied up on the couch between Grandmother and Grandpa and watched TV until the cartoon *La Calabacita* came on the screen.

La Calabacita broadcast across the country nightly at 8 p.m., and every Cuban child knew when they heard the soothing lullaby and saw an animated magical little pumpkin sprinkle fairy dust on sleepy children, it was bedtime.

"Vivianis," Grandmother said in a serious tone. "Tomorrow, we are going to call your mother. She has some news for you," she said.

I nodded.

Mother had been in the USA since I was four years old. I loved her, but she felt more like an auntie than a mother.

I kissed my Grandparents goodnight and fell asleep dreaming about my parents.

II – MOMMA AND DADDY

Like Armando, I dreamed about what it would be like to have a momma and daddy under one roof.

My father was a towering figure. I'd seen photos of him and used to try to imagine the sound of his voice. He was known in town as a tough guy. He loomed over six feet tall and had trouble with his temper. But he was also an artist and had hoped to study art in Europe one day.

When people in Sibanicú said I reminded them of my father, I was never sure if it was a good or bad thing.

One time I overheard my grandmother gossiping with the neighbors, "Be careful what you say around Vivianis, because she may turn out to be like her father." It sounded like a bad thing to turn out like my father. But I can see why my mother fell in love with him. He was broody, athletic, and loved her fiercely. Mom was a petite woman who was always on trend. When I was a kid, she wore thick chunky high heels with overlined lips and thin eyebrows. She dyed her hair red.

Before they started dating, Dad was always with his brother. Dad's nickname was *El Blanco*, and his brother was *El Negro*.

The two brothers had a reputation for roughing people up and picking fights. After Dad fell in love with Mom, that all stopped. My family told me there was some worry about their relationship, since Dad was known for being a violent man.

When my mother became pregnant with me, my father was so happy.

Mom, who was very young, only twenty, was in her first trimester and when our neighbors started yelling " *¡Liudmila, corre se van a matar!*" (Run Liudmila, they are going to kill each other!)

My uncle and father got into an argument and then a fistfight.

I don't know what was said between the two of them. I don't know how or why it ever became so violent, but I do know that in a matter of minutes, my uncle had stabbed my father with a fatal wound.

He died that day.

Twenty years old, a new baby girl, and suddenly, she was without her husband.

Making a living in Cuba as a single parent was really difficult, but Mom was entrepreneurial, a big thinker. She would hitchhike across Cuba to cities like Santiago de Cuba and La Habana to buy staples in bulk, such as coffee, cheese, shampoo, and toothpaste. Then, she'd take the goods back to our hometown and sell the items in the market.

In my early years, it never felt like we were poor because Mom always made sure we had more than enough, but life was difficult on her.

Thankfully, when I was age four years old, Mom's luck was about to change.

Before he passed away, my father had applied for the Diversity Green Card lottery program to the USA for our family. America used to randomly draw names and invite people from certain countries to apply for a visa. My mother's name was drawn from the lottery.

God was working in the background the whole time.

A few months later, Mom packed up a few small pieces of luggage and moved to the USA. Of all the places, she chose to relocate to Houston because she didn't want to go anywhere cold.

I had to stay behind with my grandparents, while Mom worked odd jobs here and there to establish herself in the new country and make a go of her own American Dream.

I missed my mother, but I was too young to be aware of what was happening. The longer she was gone, her memory faded, but I could always smell the sweet scent of her perfume on the gifts she'd send me.

Mom couldn't visit often. It was a year before she came back home. I remember thinking, *She looked so pretty and modern.* She had a new haircut and was wearing beautiful new clothes.

Every time she visited, she'd give me a huge hug. Then she'd unzip her large suitcase, which was stuffed with American clothes and toys. I was always very popular with the neighborhood kids when Mom visited. They were so curious about the USA and especially about my new fandangled toys.

Then Mom would go back to the States and leave her sweet sugary smell behind.

III – PHONE WALKS

I woke up to the natural soundtrack of Sibanicú. Roosters crowing, men calling out in the street selling their bread, and neighbors gossiping in Grandmother's kitchen over cups of coffee.

By the time I got out of bed, Grandmother had already cleaned the entire house and entertained the entire block of women.

Grandpa had left for work. He was an incredibly thrifty man. He once made me an abacus out of little pebbles.

"Ready, Vivianis? Put on your shoes," instructed Grandmother. I hated wearing shoes, but I obeyed.

Our family didn't have a phone. Most families in our neighborhood didn't even have a landline let alone cell phones. So, whenever we wanted to connect with my mother, we'd need to ask our friends on the other side of town to use their phone. It was a few miles away, and we didn't have a car, so Grandmother and I hopped on our bicycles.

Traffic in Sibanicú consisted of bicycles, a few cars here and there, and even horses. We didn't have a stoplight in the city, but everyone knew how to share the dirt roads.

"We're going to make a quick stop," said Grandmother, calling to me from her bike.

We turned left on a narrow street. I followed behind and watched lush green scenery and colorful homes pass by.

"Ok, let's stop here," Grandmother said and parked her bike behind a large tree. I did the same.

"Come here, stay close," she whispered.

We were in front of a teal house. And as we approached the house, Grandmother suddenly stopped and cursed under her breath in Spanish.

"Ok, let's go."

At first, I was confused, but then I saw my Grandfather's company car around the side of the house.

Later I'd learn he had been carrying on an affair for years with the woman in the teal house. My Grandmother knew about their relationship, but that didn't stop him.

Once, I overheard them arguing, and he said, "The only reason I'm still here is for Vivianis." And you know what? He was telling the truth. Years later, my Grandfather left my Grandmother and married the woman in the teal house. They are still married to this day. Grandmother never took on another husband; for her, there was only one man.

After they separated, their relationship became so much more amicable. Today, they have a sweet relationship. Even though he moved on with his life, Grandfather still pays daily visits to Grandmother. I don't think he ever stopped loving her.

We continued on to a friend's house and paid a few cents to use their phone. Mom was on the other side of the line.

In between the phone calls, we'd write mother letters. I was too young to even know how to write my own name, but I'd dictate my messages to Grandmother, who would always sign the letters with a heart and, "From your precious daughter, Pearl."

Grandmother punched the numbers in the corded phone and let it ring. She spoke to Mom for a few minutes before handing me the phone.

"*Hola, mi princesa*," said Mother.

Her voice was as sweet as her perfume.

"*Princesa*, I want you here with me in America. Ok? It's time for you to come here," she said.

I was frozen. I didn't even know what to say.

"I have a special room for you, your own bed, your own clothes, all prepared for you," she continued.

"And I am sending Jose down to pick you up and bring you here."

I don't know what she said next because my mind was already spinning with anticipation. It was time to leave my friends and family and start a new life in the USA.

IV – GOODBYE BIRTHDAY PARTY

On the day of my eighth birthday, I decided to dress up in my blue Cinderella costume and tiara. That afternoon my friends and family came to the house for my party. It wasn't just a birthday celebration; it was a going away party.

After I blew out the candles on my cake and gave my friends hugs goodbye, I went into my bedroom and packed one suitcase. Mom had said not to bring too much. She would have brand new things for me in America.

"Ready to go?" Jose asked. His shadow hung in the doorway of my bedroom.

I didn't know how to respond. I wanted to be with Mom, but I also didn't want to leave my grandparents.

I zipped up my suitcase, took off my princess outfit and changed into a comfy tracksuit. Like Cinderella, I was ready for my fairytale to begin.

I hugged my grandparents and cried when we said goodbye.

"Pórtate bien," said Grandmother.

"We will write to you," said Grandfather.

Then we settled in the car and headed to the airport. It was pitch black outside. In Cuba, there aren't many streetlights. I wanted to see my neighborhood one last time, but I could only see outlines of buildings in the black night sky. As we drove, I closed my eyes and pictured my friends and all of the adventures I had had.

The airport was the farthest point I had ever traveled in my life, and it was just the beginning of the journey. The more I thought about how far away I was from my grandparents, the sadder I became. I burst into tears.

"Do you want to go back?" asked Jose from behind the driver's seat.

I didn't say anything, only sniffed and wiped my tears.

"Tell me right now, and we can turn the car around," Jose said, sternly.

It sounds wild, but this man was not bluffing. I knew that if I said turn around, he would do it. And I also knew, if I turned around, I would go back to a smaller life.

Something inside of me felt like there had to be more. I thought about the painting with the blueberries and the strawberries, Mom's sweet perfume, and the life she was trying so hard to make for me. I couldn't let Mom down.

"No," I said, "Don't turn around."

I don't remember the flight, only that the sky was so black. I fell asleep and woke up in America, where trouble was waiting.

VI – I'D LIKE TO BE AN AMERICAN

The first place we went when Jose and I got off the plane was the great American burger joint Wendy's. That's where my mom was pulling a double shift. When we walked into the fast-food chain, she ran from behind the counter and handed me a huge teddy bear.

"Hola *princesa*, I am so glad you made it!" she said and kissed me again and again.

I was in awe of everything, starting with the Wendy's menu that had so many different choices. I hadn't even seen a hamburger in real life at that point, let alone a Jr. Bacon Cheeseburger!

When we finally arrived at Mom and Jose's one-bedroom townhouse, she walked me up to my bedroom.

"This is all for you, mi *princesa*," she said proudly.

I toured the little room. There was an air mattress on the ground next to the wall, which I thought was the coolest thing ever, thinking it was filled with water because it was so squishy.

Mom had decorated my room in pink and princess themes.

"Pearl, America is very different from Cuba," she said with an air of seriousness. "You can't go outside by yourself. We don't know everyone," she said.

I understood.

At that time, I didn't speak a lot of English, and I definitely didn't understand what people were saying to me. So, those first few weeks, Mom would take me to Wendy's and leave me in the office while she'd work her doubles.

Then the new school semester started. By that time, I was so excited to meet other children my age.

The night before school, I laid out my outfit and braided my hair so it would be crinkly the next day. My hair was super long, well past my bottom.

That morning Mom registered me at the front office of the bright orange school, and then the principal walked me into my new third grade class. I was so nervous.

I walked across the room to where the teacher was sitting. All of the students quieted down and observed me. I heard a few whispers.

The teacher was a bald white guy and when I greeted him in Spanish, I attempted to give him the traditional *kiss, kiss, kiss* on the cheek, which is what I always did with elders in Cuba.

But before I could even give him one kiss, he recoiled quickly in his seat, and said in Spanish, *"¿Que haces?"* (What are you doing?)

All the children exploded in laughter.

"I'm giving you a kiss," I said back in Spanish, so confused.

"We don't do that in the USA," he said flatly. "Go take a seat."

I was mortified. With one simple action, I became the social pariah of the fourth grade.

Most of the other children spoke English and Spanish since most of them were of Mexican descent, but they would act like they couldn't understand me when I said something to them in Spanish. Because of the way they treated me, I made a vow to myself to never marry a Mexican.

God has a funny sense of humor, doesn't He.

Sadly, my school experience would only become more difficult from there. No one wanted to make friends with me. Later that day, the kids started teasing me about my long hair.

After a very lonely lunch spent by myself, I came back to my desk and discovered a bunch of cruel notes written by boys and girls in my classroom.

"Go home. You're an idiot. You are ugly. Kill yourself." Written in Spanish, so I could understand.

They'd written that I looked like the little girl in the movie *The Grudge* or *The Ring*, both of whom have super long dark hair.

My heart sank into the pit of my stomach, and I hid behind my long hair.

I was once so proud of my hair. It was dark and thick and always clean but in the USA, it was a source of shame.

I came home and burst into tears.

"What's wrong, *princesa*!" my mother asked.

I told her about the bullying that occurred over my first few weeks of school.

"Don't worry," she said. "You'll get through this. Just keep your head down. You don't need them. They are probably just jealous," she said.

Her words were futile when it came to surviving an entire day of school, which seemed to stretch until eternity.

Especially recess.

Most kids look forward to recess unless you don't have a friend, then you dread it.

During those first few weeks of school, as other kids would play games with their friends, I chose to go sit in a bathroom stall to kill time.

When the bell rang, I came out of the bathroom stall and was met by an angry mob of girls from my class.

"Why do you wear your hair like that, you freak?" said one of the larger girls.

I stared back at her. Blood rushed to my head.

Another girl pushed me up against the wall.

"You should cut all of this ugly hair," she said.

I didn't say anything. I looked her dead in the eyes.

Thankfully, a teacher walked into the bathroom before anything progressed. But that's when I realized even the bathroom was not a safe place for me.

So, the next day at recess, I chose to sit underneath a tree by myself.

Under my tree, I watched the other children play together. Soon, without even realizing what I was doing, I started talking to my dead father.

"Dad, I know you're not here on Earth, but I know you can hear me," I said. "Dad, help me get through this day. If you were here, you would fight for me."

At the time, I wasn't a Christian, so it never occurred to me to pray to Jesus. I didn't know there was a Heavenly Father keeping watch over me through my darkest moments. So instead, I would talk to my earthly father.

Throughout that year, I experienced heavy sadness for the first time in my life. I couldn't contain all the sadness in my chest, but I couldn't let the other girls see me cry.

After surviving the first few weeks of school, I began writing vulnerable letters to my Dad. Mom couldn't help me, but maybe my father could intervene. I wrote those letters in my journal well into my adult years, and I saved them.

Dear Dad,

Dad, today was another really hard day. The kids said I should kill myself. Maybe they are right. I don't know. Mom works so hard, and she is never at the house. And there's no one here for me. Cuba is so far away. I miss it so much. I miss you so much. Thank you for listening, Daddy. I am going to go to sleep now. Please watch over me.

-Pearl

I closed my journal when Jose called me into the living room.

Mom and Jose's relationship was hot and cold. At some point they had broken up and we had moved into our own one-bedroom apartment.

I remember he showed up to our door and sweet talked my Mom into letting him come inside.

Out of the blue, Jose suggested we all pick up and move to Tampa, Florida.

"Let's get a fresh start," he said to us. Jose's sister and her family lived in Tampa. He suggested we live with her for a while until we could get our own place.

Nothing could be worse than dealing with the hideous school kids, I thought.

So, I was all for the move. *Get me out of Houston*, I thought. *I'll try to start over. I won't kiss the teacher this time, and I'll be cool.*

"Fresh start," said Jose, looking at me.

"Yes! Mom, please please please let's move!" I begged.

Mom agreed. A fresh start would be nice.

So, she started a relationship back up with Jose that day, and we prepared to move.

We packed up a U-Haul truck, drove across the country, and moved into Jose's sister's home. The exterior was bright white, and we were cramped on the inside, but I was elated to be out of Texas.

One of the first days in Tampa, Jose and I were in the garage unpacking boxes while Mom was out at the grocery store. He was in a mood.

"Help me with this," he barked.

For some reason, his tone pushed me to my limit. I wanted to be stronger in Tampa. Have a real fresh start. Be bolder, and not take any guff from anyone anymore.

"You're not my father," I said directly.

Jose's face turned red. "Get over here now," he growled.

I instinctively backed up, and he pushed my shoulder. Then, I lost my balance and fell to the ground.

When I looked up, he was towering over me, taking off his belt.

He took me to the bedroom at the end of the hall and made me take off my pants so he could spank me like a small child. He beat my bottom so hard it bruised.

When my mother came home and found out what had happened, she went through the roof. She had never raised her hand to me.

"That's MY daughter!" she screamed, "How dare you! If you ever touch her again, I'll kill you!" she screamed.

After that, there was a rift in their relationship for months. We continued as an odd little trio, each living our own individual life.

Shortly after the spanking incident, I was alone with Jose, unboxing our items again. No one else was home.

"Pearl," he said, edging closer to me. "Do you?"

"Do I what?" I asked.

"Do you ever..." he trailed off.

I continued unboxing my things. I pulled out the teddy bear Mom had given me when I arrived.

"Nevermind, it's stupid," he said.

I hugged the teddy bear. It still smelled like mom's perfume.

"What?"

He walked up to me and put his hand under my shirt.

"Do you ever touch yourself?" he asked.

I dropped the teddy bear.

I was nine.

CHAPTER 3

Armando

McAllen, TX - Corpus Cristi, TX

Do not be deceived: Bad company ruins good morals.
—1 CORINTHIANS 15:33

I was educated by the school of YouTube.

The internet wasn't only my escape, it was my professor in the school of life.

As a child of the late 1990s and early 2000s, I was always connected to the Net. Back in the 2000s, the internet was full of possibilities. I was chatting on MySpace and entering chat rooms before I ever had a smartphone. My first friends were manufactured online behind screen names, and the avatar I had created for myself was a look I couldn't achieve in my wildest elementary school dreams. It was all fake.

Instead of being glued to Nickelodeon and Cartoon Network like Gen X or older millennials, my generation was glued to YouTube.

YouTube started as a home for funny videos like *The Star Wars Kid, Stomping Grapes, Charlie Bit My Finger,* but it evolved to become a platform for larger-than-life personalities who gave rise to the word vlogging. I was totally mesmerized by vloggers—especially fitness vloggers.

Do you want to be fit? There's a video for that. Don't know how to pick up chicks? No problemo, there's a video for that. Want to learn how to ace an English test? There's a video for that. How about how to get a girl to sleep with you? Definitely a video for that, too.

Before I came to be a believer in Jesus, before scripture, other believers, and a relationship with Jesus became my guide, I followed a roadmap for success on YouTube.

By the 2000s, there was an onslaught of business bros and gym rats creating content targeting dudes just like me.

I had moved in with my Dad in the ninth grade with so much hope for a meaningful father-son relationship. But unfortunately, Dad wasn't ready to connect with his sons.

I found living in his house as isolating as my mother's. What's worse, the more my father ignored me, the angrier I became.

It was my first year of high school in McAllen, and I was already deep into my disordered eating habits. By then, I realized I didn't want to just be "skinny," I wanted to be buff and in shape, like my YouTube heroes.

When I started school that semester, I felt like a whole new person. I left my chubby little kid body and transformed myself into a sleek and fit guy. No longer 200 pounds, I was probably about 160, and was doing the "Insanity" fitness program in between selling merch out of my backpack. For a kid, I was making bank!

When I wasn't hustling, I threw myself into sports. Gradually, I traded video games for real games that could get tangible results in my body.

After school, I'd go to the gym to avoid being at home alone. I was so sick of being by myself. The more my father ignored me, the more I developed resentment for him. He had married a new woman who took up all his time. I loved my stepmom, but I wanted my dad's attention.

When my father did try to parent, or tell me what to do, I responded in anger. One time my father caught me coming in way past curfew and told me off.

"You're no one to me," I said. "What makes you think you can just act like my father when you weren't there for me the last ten years?"

The fight escalated, and I stormed off to my room.

That night I snuck out of my window and escaped to hang out with my friends—something I had already done several times that year.

I was growing into a young man who didn't respect authority, didn't respect women, and didn't respect myself. My attitude was in the toilet. I was like a wild bronco who wouldn't be tamed.

Not surprisingly, I gravitated toward a rough crowd. Hustling my fitness products was making me money, and all that money went directly to drugs and alcohol. I didn't need to spend money on video games with fake friends when I could drink beer and get high with real friends. Eventually, I'd escape into the fogginess of a high or the stupidity of drinking. When you go looking for trouble, you find trouble. And on the days you don't, trouble finds you.

II – CHOLO LIFE

Given how close McAllen is to the Mexico-US border, many of my classmates had family members with ties to both countries. I first noticed this because of a kid with brand-new shoes. They must have been over 200 bucks, and I knew his family didn't have that kind of money. So, I struck up a conversation with him, and we bonded over music.

I found out his father was part of a Mexican cartel. I hung out with other kids with ties to the cartel, and this kid introduced me to the Mexican Cholo life. The boys were only in ninth grade, but they had the street smarts and swagger of any adult. They were biding their time in school while aspiring to be drug dealers and part of a gang.

Gang life appealed to me. It sounded like a family. There was structure, a hierarchy, and a brotherhood I was craving.

I started listening to their music and smoking weed with them after school in a nearby park. They'd tell me about the life their fathers were living back in Mexico. The way they spoke about their fathers, they lionized them. Looked up to them. Plus, they always were decked in the trendiest clothes. They wore oversized designer hoodies, gold rings, True Legend pants, Armani, and expensive watches and shoes. Guys like this want to stick out. They've felt like they've been on the outskirts of society for most of their lives and lean into it. They make a brotherhood out of loners.

They had a language, a slang too—like bad Spanish. I picked up a lot of nasty behaviors from these guys and started down a path of desensitization to violence and sex. We'd watch hideous videos of cartel hits. Disembodiment, people being set on fire, and some things too evil to even write. All of us cheered for the cartel as we watched. The vibe was always: *Those idiots deserved it, they were on the wrong turf, or, he stole from the cartel and got what he earned.*

But when we talked about gang initiation, things started to get real.

To become initiated, you'd have to take a heavy beating from a group of guys. If you survive, you're in, and if you don't, well, you don't. It didn't sound great.

Dad knew I was going down the wrong path. He could see it on my face and the growing harshness of our interactions.

Thankfully, God had better plans for my life. One day Mom called Dad in a panic.

"I want the boys back," she said.

I found out years later Mom had been suffering from depression, and when we went to live with our dad, she felt like she had no purpose. She nearly took her life.

Dad must have sensed the urgency in her voice. That, and he was concerned about me getting involved with a gang. So, we literally packed up everything in a day and moved across the state to live with Mom again.

III – TOXIC PATTERNS

Now back in Corpus Christi, I was entering my sophomore year with the kids I knew in middle school. But this time I was returning as someone who was not only physically different, but emotionally different as well. I had been running with a rough crowd and had saved up a little money from my side hustles. I walked into high school with an attitude of confidence, like I owned the place.

When I showed up for orientation in the school auditorium, all the kids I knew from middle school were already seated. I walked in the doors and heard everyone cheering!

"Armando! Is that really you?" someone shouted as I walked confidently to an empty seat. I looked over recognizing a couple of the guys.

"No way, dude! You changed so much! Yo! It's Armando!" one of them said in awe and motioned for me to sit with them.

It felt great.

I settled into a seat next to guys who wouldn't have given me the time of day in the past. They all nodded and shook my hand.

Then I felt a tap on my back. I turned around, and it was the girl from English class who made fun of me for smelling so bad years earlier.

"Hi," she said bashfully.

I nodded.

"You look different," she said.

I nodded again and sat back in my seat, smiling to myself. That's when I realized these new looks could not only get me new friends but also girls. I had never asked a girl out in real life— only my RuneScape girlfriend, Skyler.

So, when I came home from school that day, the first place I went to was YouTube. I typed in, "how to ask a girl out." Naturally, I found a slew of videos. There was one channel called "Real Social Dynamics" with a polarizing figure. This guy would give advice to young men on how to sleep with women. Videos also instructed viewers on how to gain control over a woman by using psychological tricks and verbal abuse. It's not surprising that this channel did not age well.

Unfortunately, when I was between eighth and ninth grade, I lapped up the videos and others like this. In a chaotic life, you're looking for things to control, and as a kid, there's a limited number of variables you can wield power over. I didn't just want girls for sex, I wanted to control them from the inside out. I wanted to be God.

Over time, I traded control of food and my body for control over a girl's body. I'd research things like "how to get girls to beg for you and how to get girls to bow down and worship you." I'd soak up the information like a playbook, watching video after video.

Not all the advice was toxic. Some videos explained how to deal with the social anxiety of looking a girl in the face and asking her out on a date for the first time.

"Alright, guys, listen. You gotta warm her up before you ask her out," the videos would say.

"Go to a convenience store, say hello to a random person, look them in the eye, and have an informal conversation. Use that experience to build confidence so you don't feel frozen when you make small talk with her." *Ok, ok*, I'd think. Then I'd go follow the playbook.

Next, the video would say something like, "You need to scream really, really loud. Let all these anxieties out in the form of a roar." So, of course, I roared. (Probably freaked out my neighbors). But man, did I roar.

Then, the videos would say: Go to the mall and ask random girls out if you have no interest in dating. That way, you can learn how to talk to not-important girls before you get to the one you really like.

So, I did just that. Essentially, I built an internal checklist on how to ask a girl out until finally, I had enough confidence to ask my real crush out.

I passed her in the hallway at school and casually said, "Sup, Lilly."

"Hi, Armando," she smiled.

"Where are you headed?" I asked.

"I'm going to go sit on the bleachers with some friends from class," she said.

"Do you mind if I walk you there?"

Pause.

I was sweating. *Be cool, man.*

"Of course. Come on," she said. And we walked together—I felt ten feet tall.

"In case you get lost, here's my number," I said and handed her my number. (Ok, cheesy, I know, but it worked!) She called me and became my first girlfriend.

We started texting at night back and forth and after a few months, I figured it was time to draw on the lessons I had learned on YouTube. *How do I get her to sleep with me?*

I sent her a text.

What are you up to?

She wrote back: *Hanging out on my own at my house.*

I wrote: *Do you mind if I come over?*

And I added a winky face ;)

She wrote back: *Sure, ;)*

So, in my kid brain, I think, *Ok, she's down!*

Then I texted: *When I come over, do you want to have sex?*

Crickets.

Nothing.

No response.

Everything in me wanted to text, "JK! JK! Just kidding," but I didn't. She broke up with me then and there.

From that point, I grew a thick skin, and I went on the hunt for someone who *was* down. From the videos, I learned not to waste your time on girls who don't want to have sex; there are plenty of other girls out there who are down.

In no time, I found a random girl and followed the formula.

Looking back, it makes me sick to my stomach. The content I was digesting was a recipe for how to hurt a woman, not how to love a woman, and it was definitely not meant for a kid my age. And to be clear, it is not meant for anyone of any age.

The guys in the videos would say, "Bro, you gotta call her a dog and a whore if you want her to want you." I consumed hours of this sludge, and it had an effect on my core. I was becoming unempathetic and desensitized. I saw women as objects and good for only one thing—sex. I carried these sentiments with me for a long time, and it would take the power of the Holy Spirit to break free from that way of thinking.

IV – PARTYING

The next lesson from my YouTube curriculum was about how to party. For the next two years of high school, I had completely transformed from a shy quiet kid to an outgoing macho dude. I was still selling fitness programs out of my backpack and making enough money to buy as much drugs and alcohol as I could smoke and drink.

This made me popular with high schoolers and even college students.

I didn't want to be at home in a lonely house, so I'd stay out as long as I could with my friends. Weekends were built for bonfires and house parties. That's where I would meet college kids, and that's when things could get pretty out of hand.

One party I'll never forget took place at my friend Ben's apartment. I got there, and everyone was already really messed up—weed and coke, the whole deal. And I am taking it all in stride.

"You want some coke, bro," Ben asked.

I stuck to weed.

As the night progressed, I realized my phone was stolen. I had sat my phone down on a table next to this long-haired dude who was high out of his mind. So, I was pretty sure he was the thief.

When I told Ben, he decided we were all going to go on a road trip to this long-haired dude's house to rescue my phone.

Five of us piled in Ben's car. I was in the backseat with two drunk dudes passed out on either side of me. Ben hit the gas, and I immediately regretted my decision to get in the car. He was really high on coke and driving like 110 miles per hour.

From the back of the car, I prayed for the first time since I was a kid, "Lord, please don't let me die tonight."

The speedometer was going higher and higher, and my heart was pumping. The other guys had no idea what was happening. Then Ben pulled out a bag of weed and a bag of coke from under his seat. I guess to show it off? He tossed it back to me. I tossed it back to him.

Finally, I saw the blue and red glow of police lights and heard the siren.

Ben pulled over. I was relieved but realized we were facing a new problem. We had enough drugs in the car to get a football team high. I prayed again. *Lord, please, I want a future. I don't want to go to jail.* That was the first time I thought seriously about my future.

Somehow, Ben completely transformed from manic high guy to a straight responsible guy. He told the officers he was the designated driver and was trying to get us home as quickly as possible. He motioned for the cops to take a look at the two guys passed out in the back seat sitting on either side of me.

I gave the officers a half smile as they looked through the window.

"I've been in your situation. I know where you're coming from," the officer said.

We were all holding our breath.

"Alright, boys, get home safely," he said. And left us with a warning.

I was shocked.

After the police drove off, Ben peeled out and started speeding again. I had learned my lesson, but I guess he hadn't.

He drove us to the home of the long-haired guy who had stolen my phone. *All this drama for a stupid phone.*

When we walked in, I saw the guy passed out on the couch holding my phone. I managed to carefully swap out my phone and then bolted with Ben and the other guys.

By the time we got back to Ben's house it was morning. If this is what college was going to be like, I wondered if I'd survive. I called my mom to pick me up from the house and had a long ride back home, thinking about my future.

V – WALMART

Unfortunately, the messaging I was absorbing through YouTube about women translated to how I viewed my own mother. On a baseline level, I despised her. Even when she brought me something to eat from a take-out restaurant, I'd scoff at her.

As I grew into a young man, I learned how to weaponize my anger. I'd use it like a grenade, throwing it at whomever was in my way.

I had spent years inadvertently studying my mother. I knew her triggers. I knew exactly what to say to hurt her. And I remember the day I decided to go for the jugular.

"You're a garbage mother," I said to her one morning, when she left a bag of Jack in the Box on the dining room table.

I was so done with the latchkey kid lifestyle. I craved a home and a real family instead of these one-off men who were still cycling in and out of our home.

"Don't you dare talk to me like that," my mother hissed back.

"I don't want this junk food," I responded.

"Ok, that's it. You're not going to SPI. That's over. Forget about it. You're going to Christian camp for Spring Break," Mom said.

I had planned to go to South Padre Island with my friends that coming summer. So, there was a huge argument, but in the end, I wound up going to church camp. I wish I could tell you that's when I started to really understand how awesome our God is and how He was working behind the scenes to protect me through all the madness but unfortunately, nothing was on my radar except surviving school and sleeping with girls.

So, at the chapel, while the worship was going on, I'd look around at the girls and decide who was going to be my next girlfriend. I even managed to get a few phone numbers that week.

I came back from the youth group unchanged and unmoved. Mom was hoping for a miracle around my behavior. But her hopes were undermined by the fact that I returned to yet another man in the house. Why should I have to change my behavior if my own mother is living "in sin," I'd think.

At that time, my Mom's boyfriend, Fernando, had moved in with us. He used to host a radio show and had a deep announcer voice with a thick Mexican accent.

I hated being around him and Mom. I'd go from school to gym to school to gym to party, party, party, repeat repeat, just to stay out of their way.

Fernando must have picked up on how badly my words were making my mom feel, as he decided to step in and try to boss me around like a father. At this point—midway through high school—I wasn't going for it.

So, Fernando took a different approach. He decided to micromanage my brother and me. But having gone so many years taking care of ourselves, we totally clashed. The fights were nonstop. The yelling, the drama, the tears, and the disappointed looks on my mother's face—it was years of hell.

Finally, Fernando had had enough of it all, and he decided to start charging me rent to live in my mother's house. Mom must have been so desperate to control me, she let it happen.

Of course, I bristled. I would yell: *This isn't even your house! Are you going to start paying rent, too?*

Fernando was relentless. He made my brother and I start paying for food, clothes, soap, etc. Everything.

He was like: *If you're going to complain about the food, then you can buy your own food.*

I wouldn't come home for days. Whenever I did return and found a rare moment alone with my mom, I'd beg her to leave Fernando.

I'd say, "Mom, he treats you like crap. Why are you just taking it? Why are you letting this guy walk all over you, and why are you letting this guy charge your sons rent to live in their own home?"

Then mom got pregnant, and I realized this dude was going to be in the picture longer than the other guys.

I wound up getting a job at the restaurant chain Cheddars to pay for rent and food. I didn't have a car, so I'd walk to work about four miles in the Texas heat. It was brutal, but hey, anything was better than being around Fernando.

After the police encounter with Ben, I tried to curb my partying. I didn't want to end up like another deadbeat, but I didn't have a good vision for what kind of man I'd want to be in the future. My grades were trash, and I had no idea what I was going to do with my life past high school. It was hard to think beyond the day, let alone a year. I was becoming more hopeless, and I began to find comfort in drinking alone.

One morning my mom was driving my brother and me, and she handed me a box from the front seat.

"This is for you," she said. I opened it to discover my favorite cologne. I was touched and thought maybe she wanted to mend things.

"Do you have money for it? It cost fifty dollars, so you owe Fernando and me fifty dollars," she said.

I sighed. I was disappointed and then became furious.

"I don't have the money," I said back to her.

"Well, Fernando is going to expect the money," she said as she kept her eyes on the road.

"Well then, I don't want the stupid cologne. Keep it."

My Mom completely flipped out. She stopped the car in the middle of the highway and started driving to McAllen.

"Mom, what are you doing?" I was panicking. I'd never seen her quite like this. "Where are we going?"

"Nothing has been the same since you came back," she howled. "You're a mean and nasty boy, and YOU are the problem. I regret having you. Everything starts to go to hell when you're here!" she screamed as the car swerved into a Wal-Mart parking lot.

"Get out! Get out! Get out!" She opened the door and pulled me out of the car.

I wasn't sure what was happening. It was all so fast. In a matter of seconds, she peeled out of the Walmart parking lot and left me on the curb. I didn't have a phone or money. And I had no idea where I was. I went inside and walked around aimlessly, just trying to get my bearings and walk off my anger and deep sadness.

I walked behind the Walmart where there was a waterway and a canal. I stood and looked into the rushing water. I felt so worthless. Abandoned. And so angry. *What am I living on this earth for?* I wondered to myself. The waters looked inviting and for a moment, I contemplated jumping in headfirst.

That would show them, I thought. Plus, then, all this madness would stop.

"Sonny," I heard a familiar voice. "Sonny, let's go."

It was my dad.

I dutifully walked over to him and followed him silently to his car.

Mom had called Dad to get me.

I wasn't welcomed back to Mom's house, so I moved back in with Dad.

Dad didn't want to start things off on the wrong foot and knowing I was drawn to the wrong crowd, he arranged for me to live with my Grandma so I could attend a different high school. It was actually the same high school he graduated from, so I had some of the same coaches and teachers he had back in the day.

Dad didn't know that he was setting me up to encounter a man who would change the trajectory of my life forever.

VI – ROY'S CHALLENGE

I lived with my grandmother. She didn't pay me much mind. The small house was bustling with my cousins and uncles. I had to share a bed with my cousin, and we did everything together.

We'd sneak out and go to raves together too. I'd just dance and zone out during the parties, totally letting the music wash over me and fade out into the beats.

I started school in the middle of the semester, and on the first day of school a teacher asked me to introduce myself to the class. As I spoke to the class, my eyes were fixed on one girl. She was having a side conversation and not paying attention to me at all. Always one to love a challenge, I thought, *I'm going to make you notice me.* I tried to speak with her after class, but she rejected me pretty quickly. *Ok*, I thought, *I gotta level up my game.*

I asked the teacher to put me in a group project with Josie, so I could spend more time with her. The teacher must have been a romantic, because she obliged my request.

Josie invited the group over to her home to work on the assignment. It was one of the prettiest homes I had ever seen. Double doors, high ceilings, sliding back doors and an infinity pool outback. I was in awe.

Eventually, Josie and I wound up dating. I had nothing back for me at Grandma's house, so after school, I'd go to Josie's house.

Roy, Josie's stepfather, was an anesthesiologist. He didn't look like someone I would imagine to be in the medical field. He was a huge guy, super in shape, and covered with tattoos. Josie's mom was super artsy, and their home was decorated with modern art.

When we first met, Roy looked me up and down. He liked me, but he was tough. He was always sizing me up, and I could tell he wasn't so sure if I was good enough for his stepdaughter.

I got to know Roy and Josie's mom Cassie really well. I ate most dinners with their family and felt like I could actually breathe at their house. It felt safe, warm, and peaceful.

Josie and I were high school sweethearts and totally tuned out everything else but each other. By the end of high school, we had been dating for about two years and were already talking about marriage.

I had no idea what was going to happen past high school. I was still aimless, and my grades were horrible.

One weeknight, when I was nearing the end of my senior year of high school, Josie and I were snuggled up on the couch, watching a movie in the living room right off the kitchen.

Roy walked in heavily and stomped through the kitchen before opening the refrigerator.

He must have grabbed a chicken drumstick, because I could hear him gnaw at that thing and chew and chew. It was like he wanted me to hear it.

He sat at the table behind the couch and didn't greet us. He kept on chewing and staring at me. I knew he was staring at me because I could feel his eyes burning in the back of my head.

Finally, Josie said, "What, Roy? What do you need?"

Roy stopped chewing.

"Armando," he said with a laser focus.

I turned around and looked at him. "Yes?"

"What are you going to do with your life?" he asked.

"Sir?" I asked.

"Was the question too hard for you?" he asked sarcastically.

I didn't know how to respond, then finally I said, "I mean, I'll go to college..."

He cut me off. "Nope. You're too stupid for college. I've seen your grades. Plus, you got no work ethic. You come here every day for two years, you eat my food, you use my money to buy food. You barely work. You can't pay for anything. What makes you think you're going to make it in college?" he asked, raising his voice.

I saw red. And I got up off the couch and got right in this huge guy's face.

"Well, forget you, Roy!" I yelled. "I don't have to live here. I don't even have to be here. Quit telling me how to live my life," I said while my girlfriend tried to calm me down.

Finally, I blurted out, "Plus, you don't know anything about me. I'm going to do real estate. Both of my parents are in real estate. That's what I am going to do."

Then he took another bite of his chicken and started chewing again.

"Come on, dude. You can barely pass high school. How are you going to study and get your real estate license? I'll tell you what you need to do. You need to shape up and join the military. You need to join the Marines," he said, and slammed down a brochure for the Marines on the table.

I rolled my eyes.

"Oh, come on, bro. I'm not going to go out there and die. You don't even know me. I don't need this." I picked up the brochure and headed towards the front door.

"Come on, Armando, don't leave," pleaded Josie.

"I'm out of here," I said as I walked out the door.

As I exited, I heard Roy say loudly, "Yeah, well, you wouldn't make it in the Marines anyways."

I slammed my car door shut and was boiling with rage. I kept hearing his words over and over. *You wouldn't make it.* It's hard to explain why, out of all the negative words spoken over my life, those words ground into my soul so deeply. Maybe it was the culmination of being underestimated by so many adults? The expectation was that I was never going to amount to anything. I was a problem—often someone else's problem to deal with and endure.

I was sick of people underestimating me.

I turned on my ignition, and rain started pouring down—one of those torrential Texas rains that come out of nowhere and dump heaps and heaps of water on the dry land.

I flipped on the radio, and Eminem's song "Stan" came on.

The rain and the music mirrored what I was feeling inside. My anger had completely boiled over like a tea kettle on the stove.

I knew exactly where the military recruitment offices were located in McAllen, and I drove directly there.

It was sometime between 5 and 6 p.m. in the evening. It must have been closing time because the lighted sign on the door, along with the interior lights, were turned off—Air Force off, Navy off, Coast Guard off. Only one light was still lit: Marines.

I got out of my car in the pouring rain. The door was locked, and I started pounding on the door. I had worked myself up in a near frenzy. Pounding and pounding and drenched in water.

Finally, the door opened.

CHAPTER 04

Pearl

Tampa, FL

For we do not wrestle against flesh and blood, but against the rulers, against the authorities, against the cosmic powers over this present darkness, against the spiritual forces of evil in the heavenly places.

—EPHESIANS 6:12

I – IT BEGINS

While my future husband was having dustups with his family, I was adjusting to life in Tampa. Our first few months in Florida, we lived with Jose's family. His nieces and two daughters were around my age and helped me fast-track my English language skills. I really looked up to them. They were always reading books in English.

We had a few good months as a little pseudo-family. After a few months we left Jose's family and moved into our own apartment across the city.

Jose became my stepdad, and he was out of work because of a back injury. He was a bald guy who was half Puerto Rican and half Dominican. He was always in cargo khaki pants, and he was also always at the apartment. Mom was hustling at several different jobs to put food on the table, so she was rarely home. It was just me and Jose for long stretches of the day and nights after school and on the weekends.

That's when it started.

It's hard to look back and try to understand this man who was the closest thing I had to an earthly father. He treated me like a daughter, bought me presents, and took care of me and my mom. When I look back, I wonder—was he grooming me the whole time? It's hard to know what was real and what was sinister.

After the day he put his hand up my shirt and grabbed my breasts, he told me not to say anything to Mom. I didn't. As an immigrant kid, you try to keep your head down and survive to make it in America.

I'd think: *If I tell my mom, then this man will leave us. Our stability will go away. What will be on the other side?*

This is why I buried these encounters deep in my soul.

One day after school, Jose asked me to take a shower with him.

"Hey, Pearl, since I'm your dad. Let's get cleaned up together. I'll help you wash up and shampoo your hair," he said.

I didn't think it was normal, but I also was so young. I went along with it.

Of course, things didn't end with the shower. He touched me all over and also touched himself.

I felt dirtier after the shower than I did going into it.

"Remember, Pearl. You'll lose your dad if you tell your mom," he said as he toweled off his naked body.

Often something innocent would turn perverse in a matter of moments— like the game Uno.

We'd play games while it was the two of us to pass the time.

We were sitting at the kitchen table, and Jose shuffled the deck. He slid me some cards, and I fanned them out in my hand.

"Let's talk about what I will get if I win," he said, looking over his cards at me across the table.

I tensed up, not sure what he'd ask for. I tried to push the image of us in the shower together down into the pit of my stomach.

"If I win," he continued. "You have to bring me water from the fridge any time I ask for it for a month."

Relieved, I said. "Ok. And if I win, you have to buy me The Sims game," I said. The Sims was a computer game that I was hoping to have. You could build your own house and create your own avatar. You could literally build a dream experience. Like Armando and his video games, I, too, wanted a way to control my little corner of the world.

"A Sims game?" he said and scratched his chin. "Well, then I'll need something better than water," he paused. "If I win, you'll let me touch you anytime I want."

My nine-year-old brain couldn't comprehend the disgusting wager. All I could see was a chance to build my own world with The Sims game. In the game, you build dream homes with a family and a white picket fence. There are no monsters, only friends. I looked at my cards and considered the risk. Even at such a young age, I was losing reasons to want to wake up in the morning. Maybe, this would help me want to get out of bed.

"Deal," I said, and we started the game.

It was a game of chance. Each of us had seven cards. The goal of the game is to get rid of your cards by matching your cards by color and number in a discard pile. When you only have one card, you yell, "Uno."

I drew my first card, "Draw 4," it said. I picked up four more cards.

Jose withdrew his card. "Pick up 2," the card ordered me.

In a matter of minutes, I could barely hold all the cards in my hands. *Had Jose stacked the deck*, I wondered.

My stomach turned to knots as, round after round, Jose discarded his hand with ease.

Finally, there was one card left in his hand.

"Uno," he smiled.

I wanted to cry, but I kept playing. I managed to get rid of a few more cards, but I was no match for him.

He discarded his last card, won the game, and took my body over for the next four years.

The older I became, the more he escalated things sexually. There was no part of my body that was off-limits for him. He always pushed it a little more without totally taking my virginity.

Of course, you can keep one's virginity intact and steal a lot more from a little girl—innocence, happiness, confidence. He took all of that from me.

Mom was an attentive parent, though, and knew something was wrong. She'd ask me if something had happened at school, or if boys were being mean to me in class again. I'd push her away and watch Jose sweet talk her over dinners together. I had never seen my mom so happy. They had been together for ten years. She laughed and loved him deeply. How could I blow it all up?

Like many children who are victims of abuse, I thought it was all my fault. I must have done something wrong, or I must have made him want to do sexual things to me.

I'm such a freak. I'm so weird. Something must be wrong with me. I'd think. *What if he told my mother that I wanted this? How shameful would that be?* I'd think. It would break her heart. She loves this man so much. I couldn't hurt her. Plus, I knew she'd be so full of sorrow to know this had been happening under her nose. I didn't want her to ever feel like a bad mother or look stupid. It's hard to explain for someone who hasn't experienced this kind of violence. It can sound ridiculous.

Most of these encounters happened on my mother's bed. When she came home from her long day of work, I was desperate to tell her what was going on, but I never did—instead I withdrew into myself.

II – EXORCISM

The longer the sexual abuse lasted, the more depressed I became and in a few months, my grades at school were slipping. I stopped talking in class altogether. I never participated in school life and wanted to be by myself. I found it hard to relate to the other kids in my class. Some weird maturity came with the sexual violence and made me see all their problems as so trivial. How could I gossip about crushes and TV shows when my reality seemed so much heavier?

I'd look at the picture of me in my Cinderella dress on my eighth birthday and wonder where that little girl went. I was smiling in the picture but during this chapter of my life, the joy had left my eyes. I rarely laughed. I looked sullen and dark and hardly left my room. I was uncomfortable in my own house.

My mother recognized this drastic change right away. She was concerned.

"I don't know what's wrong with her. She doesn't say anything. She never talks to me anymore," I overheard Mom whisper to Jose one night.

"She's depressed. Maybe it's a demon," I heard Jose say.

I rolled my eyes. *Pretty rich coming from the demon himself.* I thought to myself.

Jose belonged to a charismatic Pentecostal church. It was the kind of church where people speak in tongues and fall out in the Holy Spirit. My mom started going with him to the church and began taking some of the spiritual concepts seriously.

"Maybe," she said.

The next day, Jose invited some of his friends from the church and a pastor to our house.

"Pearl, can you come here for a minute," my mom called.

I came out of my bedroom to a group of adults all staring at me. As soon as they saw me, they broke into prayers.

I was ambushed by an exorcist.

It was an absurd experience. They all laid their hands on me and began praying in the spirit, trying to cast out "the demon" that they believed was the cause of my depression. I wanted to shout out, "This man is the reason!

He's the demon, and he's right there!" But I kept silent. The more and more they prayed, the more ridiculous I felt. I started to laugh. Boy, did that rile them up.

"The demon is laughing at us!" They'd cry and then go into another cycle of intense prayer.

After the unsuccessful exorcism, Jose suggested I be sent away to a Christian youth group camp. It was a weeklong summer camp.

I didn't question going to camp. For me, it meant one week when I wouldn't have to be touched by Jose. So even though I was deeply shy and introverted, I was happy for the change of scenery.

At camp that week, I saw a glimpse of my old self. Away from Jose, I started to come out of my shell and make friends with my bunk mates.

It was also the first time I had really heard the Gospel. After all the games and bonding experiences during camp, we'd have a sermon and praise and worship at night. At the altar, there was a huge wooden cross. The preacher said we could take a piece of paper and nail what was on our hearts to the cross.

"Cast your cares on Him, because He cares for you," the preacher said. "Jesus takes it all and gives you a heart as white as snow," the preacher said gently, and invited us to "'cast our burdens on the cross."

I still remember what I wrote,

Lord,

Why did you let my father die? Why haven't you protected me? How could you let this man come into my life and hurt me? Please forgive me for my sins. Take the pain away.

Love,
Pearl

I took the piece of paper and nailed it to the cross. I felt lighter, and a little spark of joy came back into my soul. I felt a little hopeful when I thought about what my life would look like going forward.

But when Mom and Jose came to pick me up from camp, they had some news.

"We're getting married!" Mom said. Jose was driving and took a quick glance at me in the rearview mirror.

My whole world froze.

"When?" I asked.

"Today!" Mom beamed.

III – HOLDING ON FOR DEAR LIFE

My mom married my abuser. I only had enough time to wash my hair and put on a dress at home before Mom and Jose whisked us all to a wedding chapel.

Mom had been convicted by the Holy Spirit during my week at camp. Jose had led her to believe that all her troubles would melt away if they stopped living in sin as an unmarried couple and made their union official before God.

Mom wore a feathery white dress and invited a few of her friends to the chapel. Our family was all still back in Cuba, so most of the people in attendance were from Jose's family.

It all happened so fast. In my head, I kept trying to square it all. *Maybe, now that he's my real stepfather, the abuse will stop. Maybe, he will be a good husband to Mom. It wouldn't make sense for him to keep hurting me, right?* This is what I told myself as I walked my Mom down the aisle and take her vows with this monster.

I was on complete autopilot. I was happy for my Mom.

I saw this man as two different creatures. There was the man who made my mom happy and helped support us. Gave us a roof over our heads and provided some stability in this country. But then there was the creep.

One day he'd act like a loving father, and the next day he would hurt me all over again. And what's even harder to explain, I did care for him. I didn't think he was a bad guy. So, I hoped things would get better after they got married.

Nothing changed.

But I had changed.

I had nailed my sins to the cross, and I wanted to be a different human.

So, the next time he threw me down on the bed and tried to mess with me, I fought back. Mom was still at work, and he was on top of me on her bed.

"If you say anything, I'm going to go to jail, and you and your mom are going to be all by yourself," he taunted as he was on top of me and took my shirt and underwear off.

I felt totally repulsed and used all my strength to push him off me. Then I raced to the bathroom and scrubbed and scrubbed my body with soap until my skin turned bright red.

Later that summer, I was scheduled to visit our family in Cuba. I was over the moon to get away from home and see my grandparents. I had a beautiful summer with my family and put all my troubles out of my mind.

I tried to push all the memories down, but they'd bubble up at the most random times. I'd feel panic and disgust whenever I'd see one of my cousins sitting on their father's lap or a friend sitting on an uncle's lap. Maybe it was totally innocent, but I could never look at these relationships in the same light.

After the summer, a few days before I was meant to be on a plane back to Tampa, reality started to hit me. I couldn't go back.

I've learned since then that Satan comes to "kill, steal, and destroy," and the internal monologue that was going on in my head was *You have nothing to live for. End it all.* And I listened. I found several bottles of pain pills and downed them like candy and laid down to die. Thankfully, the Lord saved me.

I began throwing up everywhere and woke up my grandmother, who raced me to the hospital. I was in the hospital for about four days, and the narrative somehow became that I tried to kill myself because of a boy at school.

When I made it back to the US, my mom met me at the airport and hugged me so tight, weeping. She didn't want to lose me, and she couldn't stop trembling as she held me in the airport.

Jose must have known it was because of him.

When the new school semester started, there was only one teacher who recognized that something was wrong. He was a nerd like me and would give me *Walking Dead* comic books to read.

Besides the teacher, my school days in Tampa were quite isolating. But unlike when I was younger, this time it wasn't because of a language barrier—it was because of an emotional barrier. I couldn't relate to the other kids. I found a tree to sit under during free time and would talk to my dead father like I had done in Texas. I felt so different from everyone. I was used to being on my own.

Lunchtime seemed to stretch on till eternity. I'd take my lunch to the bathroom and eat on the toilet so I could avoid the shame of not having any friends.

I had to speak to a guidance counselor about my mental health.

The counselor asked me if I was having suicidal thoughts. I said yes, and the next thing I knew, I was being carted off to a hospital for mentally ill people. I spent a week there, and let's just say it didn't help me gain any friends. Now I was the loner girl who was sent to the loony bin.

Thankfully, in all of this darkness, my Mom saw that her life was not improving with Jose in it, and she broke up with him.

But then he started calling me.

IV – BURNING DOWN THE HOUSE

After Mom broke up with Jose, things were good at first. I entered high school, and we moved to a new house in Tampa. I had blocked Jose on all my social media and from my phone. But he would call my mother to speak with me. My mom had a pleasant relationship with him as the breakup ended amicably, so she'd put him on the phone with me.

I wanted to take all the abuse to the grave with me, but he kept calling and wanting to catch up. He'd say pervy things on the phone, and I started to feel claustrophobic all over again.

Even with this man out of my life, how will I ever escape him? I wondered hopelessly.

I was fourteen years old. Mom was at work and had left a lighter for her candle on the kitchen counter. We were in a new house, but the furniture was all the same from the years we lived with Jose— the same couch and beds where Jose had done all the nasty things to me. My mind was spinning.

Walking around my house, I wanted it to all disappear. I drank a little bit of my mom's Spanish alcohol left over from a party. She was never a big drinker and rarely kept alcohol in the house, but there was just enough for me to feel tipsy.

I took the lighter and held it up to our curtains for a few seconds. The curtains lit up quickly. I threw some water from the kitchen sink on them before it got out of control. The acrid smell of smoke was in the air, and the curtains were clearly ruined.

That's when I thought, *Well, I've already started this fire. Mom is going to be so mad about the curtains, and how can I explain it's because of the pain I feel inside because of Jose? Better to die with this truth.*

I walked over to my Mom's bedroom and stood over the bed where Jose had hurt me for years. I took the lighter to the mattress and watched it go up in flames.

I watched the fire dance up the walls, then spread over me to the ceiling. That's when I decided to get into the closet and stay there in the fire. I could hear the windows popping and crackling open. Soon everything went black, and my eyes were tearing from the smoke. There was so much smoke.

Just like that day in Cuba when I took all those pills, I had intended to die. But Jesus Christ had a bigger plan for me.

Something inside me said, "Get out right now," and I pushed the hot closet door open.

The smoke rose to the top of the ceiling, but close to the floor was a little smokeless pathway. I crawled on my hands and knees from the bedroom to the living room. I could barely see in front of myself, but I felt as though I was guided through the flames.

Finally, my lungs were so filled with smoke that I had to take a break in the living room. With flames all around me, I laid on the floor and felt the melted ceiling drip on my back. I could see dark gray shadows, and the smoke detector batteries turned green and crackled.

I heard a voice inside me say, "You don't want to die." I knew it was true.

I reached inside my pocket, grabbed my cell phone, and called my best friend.

"My house is on fire," I managed to say, and then I dragged myself to the front door. With all of my strength, I turned the scorching doorknob and fell through the open doorway; smoke tumbling out with me.

That's where I passed out, and that's where my best friend's stepfather found me. She and her father had raced over to my house. He lifted me away from the fire and took me directly to the hospital.

At the hospital, I could hear doctors all around me, and someone yelled, "She has too much smoke in her lungs; she's not going to make it."

They had to cut my clothes off my body, and I do remember them shoving a tube down my throat. I remember how much the tube hurt and how I couldn't swallow.

When I woke up, my hair was totally singed and black. My face was black with smoke and soot too. I touched my hair, and it was hard.

My poor mother. She was beside herself with grief. She was so thankful that I was ok.

After I was stabilized in the hospital came conversations with police. The doctors had found alcohol in my system and asked if I had started the fire on purpose.

I denied it all. The police report said the fire was due to an electrical malfunction.

Mom and I moved in with one of her close friends and because of the amount of alcohol the doctors found in my system, I was assigned a social worker who checked in on us.

Even now, it breaks my heart to think of the hard work my mother had put into making a life for us in the USA, only for it all to go up in flames. Our government papers, passports, baby pictures, and our whole life was gone.

I felt completely devastated for my mother, but I also felt so relieved to never have to see any reminders of the years of abuse. It was finally over.

Years later, she asked me if I had burned down our house. She had seen the signs. She didn't know why, but she knew me.

For many years I denied it, but finally, I told her. And with every truth I began to tell, I began to feel the dark clouds lift, just like the smoke.

V – IT ENDS

It's weird how life keeps moving forward. I burned down our house, took two weeks off from school, and then kept on going to class like nothing had happened.

I had a boyfriend. At age fifteen, we started sleeping together. I had a difficult time. Every time we slept together, I would recoil and cry.

He asked me what was wrong, and finally, I told him everything about Jose. He was the first person I told. I also told him how I had attempted to take my life.

It was probably a lot for a high school boy to handle, but he was sweet.

We dated for about two years, but when he broke up with me, I thought my world had ended.

I couldn't imagine my life without this guy. He was the only one in the world who knew the truth.

It was a perfect storm because Jose was also back in town. I was working at Burger King, and he showed up out of the blue. Seeing him completely rattled everything in my soul. I couldn't deal, so I ran away.

I had no plan. I was gone for two days. Mom had to call the police.

For a full day, I didn't eat, and I slept outside.

Finally, my mom called my boyfriend and asked him to help find me.

"Why would she do this?" My mom asked him on the phone.

"I don't want to say anything, but it has to do with her stepdad. You should ask her," he said.

I wasn't hiding far from home. In fact, I was in my neighborhood. My boyfriend searched all night, and he found me the next morning.

When I came back to Mom, she welcomed me like she had so many times before. But this time she sat quietly next to me and said, "What did Jose do to you?"

I burst into tears and told her everything.

She turned into a lion and said we were going to go to the police right then. I didn't want to relive any of it, but I told the police everything in one long night.

It felt like another nightmare. The police needed me to contact Jose to try to get him to confess to the sexual abuse. They said there wasn't enough evidence to charge him with anything.

I called Jose, but he didn't answer. Maybe he knew his time was up.

After that we never heard from him again. My best guess is he went back to the Dominican Republic.

My mom still blames herself for everything.

I don't blame her.

Every single thing that happened in my life brought me to where I am today. Writing this book, sharing with you. And I believe in a God who renews all things and takes the bad parts of our story and makes it beautiful. The scripture says God will bring beauty from ashes. And I know this to be true.

"And provide for those who grieve in Zion—to bestow on them a crown of beauty instead of ashes, the oil of gladness instead of mourning, and a garment of praise instead of despair. They will be called oaks of righteousness, a planting of the Lord for the display of his splendor."

—ISAIAH 61:3

That's what He did. By His mercy, my life didn't end in Cuba or in that fire. By His grace, I am here to tell you the good news of what can happen when you choose life.

VI – A HEART, MY PLAN, AND HIS PLAN

A year after the fire, I asked Mom to put me in a charter school. I wanted to avoid seeing people at school. But it only lasted one year.

We lived paycheck-to-paycheck and supplemented Mom's income with food stamps. I continued to work at Burger King, so my high school life wasn't nearly as exciting as Armando's. I wound up going back to a regular high school my senior year. I was so behind in school that I started taking online classes so that I could graduate with my class.

I had lived so much of my life thinking I was going to die that I never bothered to make plans for the future. Honestly, I didn't think I would live long enough to graduate high school. So, by the time senior year started, I wasn't sure what to do.

Thankfully, the new group of friends I had made were all quite driven and had plans for their futures. I was in awe of my peers who could plan five and ten years ahead. Most of them were already taking AP courses in high school to count towards their college credits. They did sports at school and studied together for exams. With this group of friends by my side, school became something I looked forward to instead of something I had to survive.

I didn't feel smart enough to go to college, and the tuition prices seemed so far out of reach. The military seemed like a practical way to fast-track your career. When I saw myself in uniform in my mind's eye, I thought, *Ill radiate confidence and strength, no one will doubt my toughness.*

The Marines had the reputation of being the most difficult branch to break into, so of course, that is exactly where I wanted to be.

I told my high school guidance counselor about my desire to join the Marines, and she thought it was a great idea. I connected with a Marine Corps recruiter and signed up.

There was one snag.

On my left pointer finger, I had a little heart tattoo. My mom had taken me to get the tattoo at a flea market when I was fourteen years old. She is covered in tattoos, so the small heart seemed pretty innocuous at the time.

Now, years later, this heart was standing between me and my dreams of enlisting because Marines are not allowed to have tattoos on their hands, face, or neck.

So, I filled out all my paperwork and began going to Saturday morning military training. I wasn't able to officially join until I had my tattoo removed, which was going to cost thousands of dollars.

After I graduated from high school, my boyfriend at the time went off to join the Marines officially, and my group of friends all went their respective ways while I was stuck at home with that stupid tattoo.

Little by little, I saved up money for the laser tattoo removal sessions. In the meantime, I enrolled in a state university online, so I could have something to keep me busy.

Over the next few years, I'd watch friends enter the military and come out in two years brighter, more disciplined, and with a clear picture of what they wanted out of life. I was envious of this kind of movement because I felt totally frozen in the same place.

Oh, but God works in such amazing ways. It took two years to remove the tattoo completely, and by that time I was already halfway through college. I lost the desire to join the military, figuring I should stick to my studies and graduate from school.

That little heart had kept me out of the Marines, which led me down the road of giving my heart to the Lord and starting my greatest adventures yet.

CHAPTER 5

Armando

Signing up and shipping out

The Lord is not slow to fulfill his promise as some count slowness, but is patient toward you, not wishing that any should perish, but that all should reach repentance.

—2 PETER 3:9

I

While my wife was unable to enter the military because of her tattoo, my first hurdle to jump over to enlist was in the form of Sergeant Harris.

Pounding on the military recruitment doors in the storming rain, Sgt. Harris welcomed me inside.

"What are you doing? Why are you here?" he asked without a smile.

"I want to enlist. I want to be a Marine," I said, looking him dead in the eyes.

"You're scrawny. You don't have what it takes."

I was still burning with motivation and running hot after Roy's comment. So, I pushed back.

"What do I need to do to prove myself?"

He made me do pull-ups right then and there, and when he was satisfied, he let me inside the building.

I didn't know then but this would be the way my military journey would continue—with doors opening and closing.

As the rain cleared up, Sgt. Harris sat me down and had a serious conversation about my future career in the military. I told him I wanted to be a hero and go kill bad guys.

Right about then another Sergeant walked from a back office. He had overheard our whole conversation.

Sgt. Vela, "Listen, you don't want to go 'kill bad guys,' you want a career," he said warmly, like he was speaking to his own son.

Then he had me pick out Marine slogans.

I was drawn to the words: *leadership, skill, challenge, discipline, physical, fitness, and travel.*

Those words described a life that was so much bigger than the one I was living in McAllen.

After I shared my dreams of coming back to real estate one day or maybe even starting my own business, Sgt. Vela thought to himself for a minute, then said, "You might want to land as an Enlisted administrative specialist 0111," he said.

I'm so thankful for this conversation, and the real way in which Sgt. Vela talked with me. He encouraged me to learn all I could from the Marines and to work towards sustainable goals for life outside of the military. I felt seen, and for the first time, I had a sense of purpose for my future.

The next day, I went back to Josie and Roy's house.

"Is Roy here?" I asked Josie at the front door.

Josie looked at me weird and then invited me inside, "Yeah, why?"

I walked right up to Roy, who was sitting at the kitchen table. I had my military papers in my hand, and I slammed them right on the table in front of him.

"I signed up last night," I said, looking him in the eye.

My girlfriend immediately started crying.

"How could you!" she bawled.

Roy looked over the papers and said, "Well then. Let's see if you can really do this. Let's see how long you last." Then he went back to his breakfast.

A few weeks later, I graduated from high school. During the graduation ceremony, our headmaster asked the grads who were going to be joining the Air Force to stand up, and a handful of people rose. The same happened with other branches of the military, but when the headmaster asked for people entering the Marines to stand, I was the only person in my whole class who stood up. I heard someone whisper, "Ah, dude. Poor guy."

I had no idea what was ahead of me.

A few weeks later, I landed in San Diego for Boot Camp. The only thing you need to bring is your birth certificate and your button-up shirts.

When I arrived at the famous "yellow footprints," I couldn't believe it. I was standing on the iconic launch pad where hundreds of thousands of legends had stood before me.

There are three phases of training. When you walk past other platoons, you can tell which phase they are in by the way their camo uniform looks. The dirtier they are, the longer they've been there.

We come in as eager puppies, wide-eyed and curious, and we come out laser focused. You can always tell when someone is nearing the end of their training because their entire demeanor has become sullen and serious.

Boot Camp was full throttle. They buzzed our heads with old buzzers that scrape your head. It felt like they were shaving off your skin. During the initiation phase, your endurance is tested. We stood on our feet for hours doing drills, pushing our bodies and minds to the edge. The Goal was to weed out the weak, separate the sheep from the wolves. We were part of the most elite branch of the military and our uniforms were the coolest. (Sorry Airforce and Army.) Still love y'all.

When a huge drill sergeant was over top of m yelling at full volume, past arguments with my parents seemed so stupid.

I had been rebellious, and I had been living in a lonely world my whole life. I had to reach deep inside to stay focused and not let my anger take control. They taught me how to turn on a robot self. I learned to numb myself so I could take a life. They taught me how to adapt to any environment, all to protect our country.

That first week was brutal. I saw many dudes totally break down and go home. I was mentally and physically drained, but I kept hearing Roy's voice in the back of my mind, *Let's see if you can make it.*

I was not about to go home with my tail between my legs. So, I pushed forward.

The first Friday is called Black Friday. It's the day you meet your drill instructors. It was also one of the most feared days that you experience that everyone talks about when they graduate. Let's just say the grueling pain and mental exhaustion we had to endure that day could make a grown man cry.

That night we were in our squad bay, which is a large room with bunk beds. We lined up next to our bunk. We didn't want to speak because we were all exhausted and didn't want to make waves with the drill sergeant.

Drill Sgt. Garcia walked into the room and ordered us to make our beds. After all the beds were made, he told us to unmake the beds and throw everything on the floor.

Again. And again. And again.

If there was so much as a grumble or a mutter from someone, he'd stop the whole process and make us start over. And the grumbler was punished with push-ups.

After Sgt. Garcia was satisfied with how we all made our beds, he had another challenge for us.

"Take your rucksack like so," he said, grabbing a large backpack which was typically around sixty pounds. "And I want you to hold it with just your pinky," he said, balancing the bag with one finger.

It wasn't the running or the push-ups or the screaming in our faces that I saw break people; it was this pinky challenge. Every time someone dropped their bag, the clock would reset. I mean, dudes were literally crying. I was, too, because of the pain.

And then Sgt. Garcia got in my face. I didn't know why, but I knew he wanted to destroy me.

"I want to take your soul, Nava," he said with a thick Colombian accent. "I'm gonna make you bleed," he said as my pinky felt like it was literally going to fall off my hand.

If you can't handle a drill sergeant yelling in your ear, how are you going to be able to handle the sound of gunfire and hear commands when things get real?

Finally, the exercise was over.

The next morning continued with exercises like this. One was called Churro Days, where we were to roll around in the sand and hot sun and we would be covered in sweat and sand looking like a churro. We worked our bodies so hard that we ended up puking everywhere.

That night, Sgt. Garcia made us put on and take off our button-up shirts over and over, again and again and again. In my head, I thought, what the heck is the point of this? Why am I here?

I must have inadvertently given off some sort of attitude because Sgt. Garcia came over to me and started yelling in my face. He made me turn around and stare at a wall for hours.

"Stand up straight. Don't slouch. Tuck in your shirt," he'd say.

Once a grubby kid who didn't bathe for days and played video games for hours, this was such a crash course in not just perseverance, but hygiene and discipline.

Even the way you eat changes. As a Marine, you don't lean over your food, you bring your spoon full of food to your mouth while sitting up straight. Plus, you have a time limit. If you can't finish your food in the amount of time set, then you don't eat.

In Boot Camp, you live week to week. With every week I survived, I'd think I *can do one more. I survived two, now can I survive three.*

I started to find a groove around day 30.

Around that time, we took a bus to Camp Pendleton in the desert. We never knew what was coming, which was intentional. We just obeyed orders.

It's funny how in that mindset, the smallest human kindness goes so far. I remember the bus driver turned on the radio, and a new Drake song came on the speakers. It must have just dropped, because none of us had heard it before.

Our heads were down, and we weren't allowed to speak to one another, but the song gave us a connection to the outside world. And with it, a little bit of hope.

As much as our internal battle was raging, we were also learning how to work with people we'd met for the first time.

Sometimes tempers flared, emotions ran high, and fights broke out, but regardless of how exhausted we were, we had to come together and accomplish the assignment or mission of the day.

During that second phase of camp, we had tactical training where we learned how to shoot guns, how to break them down and put them back together. We learned how to disarm someone, and how to survive injuries. We also had to learn how to kill someone in hand-to-hand combat.

Suddenly I'm not the Armando who's playing video games in the utility closet, I am training with real weapons in simulations where there are grenades going off, and people shooting at me in real life. I felt good about myself after accomplishing our missions.

For three months, we were off the grid, with no connection to what was going on back home. No YouTube for me. But we did receive letters.

There was a large bag of mail, and during the second phase of training, we'd start receiving letters from back home. My parents sent me letters to encourage me to keep going.

Looking back, I understand what the point of isolation and repetition was intended for, how it grew aimless youth into people who can focus under extreme pressure. Ultimately, this training was meant to help grow us into people who would be willing to put our lives on the line for our country. I still had a lot to learn.

"YOU GOT TO PUT IN THE WORK. LOSE SLEEP. ETC. There is no secret formula. Keep grinding and believe in yourself. Don't listen to the people on the sidelines, keep doing YOU. Anyways, have a productive week beasts."

—*NAVATHEBEAST*

II – GRADUATING BOOT CAMP

"I FELT LIKE A MILLION BUCKS, because I just finished all my training, so now Motivator had nothing against me."

—*NAVATHEBEAST*

Finishing basic training was a massive accomplishment. It was the first thing I had ever done for my future. My family came to my graduation.

"Where's Roy?" I asked my girlfriend.

"He couldn't make it," she said.

I was disappointed, but then I saw my Mom and forgot about Roy. We held each other, and both of us started crying. It's hard to really put into words how I was feeling. But it was like all the crap we had been through together didn't matter. We had each other, and I could feel her love for me. I missed my family so much in those three months. I felt remorseful for the way I had spoken to my mom in the past. From then on, I wanted to be respectful and speak to her with honor. I didn't want to argue with her like a child. I felt grown.

After graduation, we went to In and Out Burger (sorry to my Texan friends, as my first love will always be Whataburger, but we were in Cali).

While I was in the restaurant, I realized I looked at my surroundings differently from the way I did before I went into the military.

I scanned the restaurant and thought, *Ok , if that guy comes up to me and tries to kill me, how could I attack him? Ok, who here is going to try to hurt us?*

In addition to that change, I also began to see slovenliness for the first time. Greasy unkempt hair and un-ironed shirts. Dirty shoes and bad posture. Things I'd never noticed but now were ingrained into my psyche as unrespectable ways to exist.

Most Marines live the rest of their lives with the standards they developed in those basic training days. It's hard to shake.

After graduation, I spent some time with Josie. She was going to culinary school in California, and I drove down to her campus to be with her for a few weeks.

One morning, around 5 a.m., her phone started buzzing. She answered, it was Roy.

He was outside the dorm.

"He wants to see you," she said, wiping the sleep out of her eyes. "He's downstairs."

I was surprised but got dressed quickly and went out to meet him. Roy was sitting in his little blue Honda Fiesta.

"Get in the car!" he said cheerfully.

The two of us drove to breakfast.

"I'm proud of you, Armando. Congratulations, you're a real Marine now," he said.

I felt proud of myself; it was a good feeling as we headed into a diner.

Roy ordered a massive amount of food for me. And as I chomped my way through the meal he watched me. "Good lord, man, slow down!" He laughed.

I was still ready to chow down after having nothing but crud at Basic for three months. But I realized he was sizing me up again like he had since I was in high school. He took a sip of his black coffee, and I could tell he wanted to say something.

"Armando, what are you going to do next? You can't be a Marine forever. It's not sustainable," he said.

I just about spit my food out of my mouth.

I had just signed up for four years and told him as much. Wasn't that good enough?

"I'm not talking about the next four years. What are you going to do with the next twenty years?" he said sternly.

I was quiet for a long time. I had an idea, but I had never spoken it aloud to anyone.

"Ok, well. I do know. But it may sound stupid," I said sheepishly.

I knew this bro would wait there for hours until I gave him an answer.

I took another bite of my food, a sip of coffee, and then came out with it.

"I want to document my life in the Marines on YouTube. No one has ever done it before. I want to be the first." My heart raced as I spit the words out. "I want to do social media. Build a career online."

"Ok, now we have something," Roy nodded. "So, let's go get you a camera."

And that's what we did. We literally left the diner, and I bought a GoPro camera.

And that is where my career in social media began.

I never saw Roy again, but I am forever grateful for the way he challenged me to want more out of life.

III – OKINAWA, JAPAN

June 3, 2017

Being out here in Japan has really taught me to get comfortable with being alone and not having moral support 24/7. Others tend to resort to alcohol, video games etc. I decided to put myself out there and produce YouTube videos, because growing up I always dreamed of doing it.

—NAVATHEBEAST

After Basic, I headed to Combat Training and then Military Occupational Specialty (MOS) School in North Carolina.

It was 2015, and it was the era of the YouTube challenge and confessional style of vlogging. So, my content fit into the zeitgeist.

I started documenting my life right away, beginning with my first day of MOS school. I vlogged about some silly food challenges. I'd carry around my camera everywhere. Other Marines were like, *What the heck is this dude doing?* I'd hear them scoff and heckle me behind my back, but I had tunnel vision. I knew I needed to keep on keepin' on.

I'd record everything.

There was a trend, "Get ready with me," that I leveraged. I'd film how a Marine gets ready for a day of work.

I was hoping to give my online audience a taste of what military life was really like, to give people access to the kind of things you only see once you've survived Basic Training. It was a life I was proud to be living. I had experienced such a radical transformation in such a short amount of time, and I wanted to share the experience with other kids who were looking for direction.

But the intersection of the military and social media was still a new territory. There hadn't been formal "military influencers" on the scene. There was no roadmap, and so I pioneered.

When I received my orders to report to Okinawa, Japan, I filmed my reaction. Japan was the last place I wanted to go, because of how far away it was from home. California and North Carolina already seemed like different words compared to Texas, but Japan? It was literally on the other side of the world. I was devastated.

I called my Mom, and she started crying. Two years across the world. And when I told my girlfriend, we realized the writing was on the wall for our relationship. It ended shortly after I left. And of course, I filmed it.

On a beach in Japan, I told my audience of about 200 subscribers about my recent breakup. It was super cheesy and over-the-top, but I wanted people to understand the strain a military life can have on relationships. I also wanted to play the field and was ready to be single. But I didn't tell them that part.

In Japan, I threw myself into my YouTube channel and began growing more and more subscribers.

The base in Okinawa slept eight people in two rooms with one shared bathroom. I was working as an administrator, pouring over a lot of paperwork. In a way, it was a typical 9-5 job, except it was in Japan, and it came with the discipline of a Marine Corps lifestyle and a strict curfew.

I'd document my days and focus on our workout routines. A lot of my videos at the time were focused on fitness.

At night I'd edit the videos. In a few months, my 200 subscribers jumped to 2,000. My roommates were so supportive and hyped me up.

My colleagues in Okinawa would say, "Hey, I saw your video, and now I am doing the workout you showed us," and it would make me feel really good knowing my videos were resonating with people.

After the workday, I'd rack my brain and think about ways I could level up my channel.

I reached out to a guy named Tim Gordon. He was working for the Air Force in Okinawa and was also documenting his experience on YouTube. He had about 80,000 followers, so to me, he was famous.

I emailed him and asked if he'd be interested in making a video together.

Marines have a curfew of 11 p.m., and since we didn't have cars in Japan, we'd take the notorious "green bus line" to get around the Island.

I pitched Tim an idea to do a Physical Training "battle" between the two of us, thinking the friendly competition between the Air Force and a Marine would make for some fun content. Tim was down.

We filmed the video for his channel, and he shouted out my channel in the video description. "Marine vs. Airman." I was pumped, but at first, the video didn't get a lot of hits.

"Hey, you win some, you lose some," Tim wrote.

But a few days later, I woke up to the sound of my phone vibrating. Then I received a text from Tim. "Dude, we're all over the news!" he wrote.

Our video got picked up by some digital news outlets and wound up going viral overnight!

"Marine vs. AirMan" was being shared all over Facebook too. In a matter of hours, my subscribers jumped from 500 to 10,000 people.

Now, any content creator will tell you that whenever you see a spike in your numbers, you gotta ride the wave. We ramped up videos to feed the machine.

I started challenging every corner of the military to take a Marine PT test. The videos were popular and gave me a reputation as "that Marine who does YouTube."

The days were long, as I'd do my regular Marines day job and then vlog and edit my videos at night. I tried to put out a video every two days. Within just a matter of months, I gained 50,000 subscribers.

Thus, Navathebeast was born.

For the first time in my life, I felt like I was exactly where I needed to be. I had found a career that made me happy and connected me with people from around the world. I felt genuinely good about myself too.

My content showed a day in the life of a Marine, and I wanted to put a positive message out there. I had felt so defeated for so much of my life, told I wasn't going to amount to anything. I wanted to change that narrative.

Unfortunately, not everyone was cool with my content. In fact, some of the most damaging comments I received during that time were from my fellow Marines. I can't even count how many times I was made fun of by my colleagues for carrying around a video camera and filming my content.

I kept my head down and continued to crank out the videos. I could hear Roy in the back of my mind: *What are you going to do after the Marines?*

This, I'd think. *Make a business through social media.*

Plus, I loved the Marine Corps, so why not continue to marry the two passions? The more I posted, the more my views and subscribers soared.

I was a sensation!

Then the higher-ups got involved. They weren't pleased with my content. I was called into a meeting with my superiors and told to immediately shut down my videos.

"As a Marine you can't be recording this!" they said.

The Marines did a full sweep of all my videos and began an investigation. The generals wanted to strip my rank. I was probably showing a little too much of the behind-the-scenes, which could be damaging. The Corps felt like it was too raw and too dangerous to show battle tactics to potential enemies.

Until that point, there were very few people filming their time in the military. This was uncharted territory, a "military influencer" didn't formally exist, so the rulebook was being written in real time.

Beyond that, it was obvious I had a split focus. And my attention to my job was called into question.

And reflecting back on that time, I think—my focus *was* split. I wasn't giving it my all. I thought I could do both, but you can't be a part time Marine. And I want to say I am so sorry for not giving this job the attention it deserved. But I kept pushing. Over two years in Japan, I grew the channel to 100,000. I was famous.

Around that time, I started a supplement company too. So, I was making videos and selling my supplements in addition to my regular Marine job.

You would think the higher-ups would be happy. I mean, I was recruiting without being a recruiter. Every day I received messages from kids who were interested in joining the military.

Still, it was stressful to wait for the higher-ups to figure out what they were going to do with me.

Finally, it clicked for the Marine Corps. They realized I could be used as an asset. A Staff Sergeant vouched for me. He fought for my case. He worked in the legal division, and he argued that my channel was doing more good for the Corps than bad. The problem wasn't the channel; the problem was my assignment. Something had to change.

IV – MARINE INFLUENCER

December 2, 2018

After enlisting in The Marine Corps and realizing not everything is handed to you, it's EARNED APPRECIATE the ones you love, especially your parents.

—NAVATHEBEAST

I was shipped off to New York in 2017. I was still on Active Duty, but I was made the first social media influencer for the Marines. It was a dream come true. I was flown all over the US to give talks to kids at local recruiting stations for the future recruit about what they could expect in their first few years in the military.

Online my content was pretty wholesome and positive. There were a lot of fitness challenges and interviews with other branches across the military from Navy SEALS, Marine Special Forces, Korean Marines, and much much more the military. I was even able to interview some of my favorite online creators. That made eleven-year-old me really, really happy.

But off-line, I was living a very different life. "Navathebeast" had taken off, and my ego was through the roof.

Those deep-seeded views I held of women from high school were still present. Now that I had found overnight fame, I became a full-blown womanizer.

Women would slide into my direct messages, and I would meet up with them for one-night stands. It became a bit of a game for me. How many different women could I sleep with in a week? I even had competitions with my roommates. We'd trade women. It got really bad.

Inside I was still the overweight kid from McAllen. And although I had developed a strong work ethic through the Marines, I didn't know how to cure my loneliness.

I had never dealt with any of my anger or grief from my adolescence. And in a way, history started to repeat itself. Just like in high school, I started focusing on fitness and girls. Only this time, I had a worldwide audience and thousands of women to choose from online.

On Saturday nights in New York, I felt like I was on the top of the world. I felt invincible. I worked around the clock on my videos and then partied most nights, living a fast life. I had no faith in God. How could I when I believed I was a god? It's a dangerous place to be.

I traveled across the country, from meet and greets with future service members to parades and parties. I was the face of the Marines. And while it was a blast to be seeing my dreams come true in real life, the job came with an emotional cost. I struggled with the title "Marine Influencer."

Should I, of all people, be the face of this institution? I hadn't seen war or served for a long time, but I was pegged for this role? Not only that, but most military life is also the total opposite of the life I was living. It's about sacrifice and service. You keep your head down and become part of a team. There is no celebrity in the military.

But my job as an influencer meant creating videos centered on only me. And since I was traveling from hotel to hotel and often rubbing shoulders with high-profile influencers, it meant showing a type of military life that really doesn't exist elsewhere. I took a lot of heat for that, and I understand why people were frustrated with my content. When someone is literally in the trenches overseas, and I am living the high life in New York, how can we both call ourselves Marines?

Looking back, those comments said behind my back—they were true. And I want to apologize for my behavior—for my attitude and arrogance.

At the same time, being a Marine meant everything to me. The discipline, the community, the institution. It made me into a man, and my whole identity was wrapped up in the military.

So, instead of addressing the haters with humility, I leaned harder into being a god. I felt untouchable, and my ego was like a wildfire burning uncontrollably across my videos and inbox.

Eventually, the military gave me a list of things I could and couldn't post online. At first, it was great, but soon the list was longer and longer, and I started to feel trapped.

Part of the appeal of being a content creator was being able to be creative and take risks online. But with the restrictions, I felt hampered, like I couldn't make the kind of videos I knew would attract new audiences. I was left with a half-hearted channel that I couldn't be super proud of, and that's when I started toying with the idea of leaving the military.

V – CIVILIAN LIFE

May 2, 2019

Life beyond the Uniform, my biggest piece of advice to all my upcoming future service members and current ones... even if you just started your journey or your 1-20 years in... start planning for the FUTURE today.

—NAVATHEBEAST

In 2019, after putting four years into my military career, I was presented with another opportunity. The Marines prepared a package for me to re-enlist. The recruiter asked where I wanted to go, Italy, Spain? Germany?

Anywhere in the world! Doing social media for the Marines.

When my work colleagues found out I was re-enlisting, they were excited for me. One guy named Sam congratulated me.

He threw a ball up and down in the air without looking me in the eyes and said, "You know what, Nava, I'm glad you're re-enlisting. Civilian life would be way too hard for you, bro. Without the Marine title, you're a no one," he teased.

His words reminded me of what Roy had said so many years earlier. And I couldn't shake them.

"What are you going to do after the Marines? You can't do this forever."

I looked through my videos that night. So many fun challenges and silly videos—a lot of motivational and instructional content too. I walked over to my mirror and looked at myself. I wasn't the fresh-faced eighteen-year-old who joined the military four years earlier. I was getting older. And I thought to myself, *man, I can't be doing these videos in twenty years.*

So, I went back to the recruiter and gave them back my package. It was August 2019, and I was ready to transition out of military life. I was ready to ask myself who I was going to be without the uniform.

CHAPTER 6

Our Stories Come Together

The thief comes only to steal and kill and destroy. I came that they may have life and have it abundantly.

—JOHN 10:10

I – PEARL

I walked behind the register of the laundromat and clocked in for a day of work. It was spring of 2019, and the days were monotonous. I was attending school online and working long hours at odd jobs.

I looked out the window and watched customers walk through the door and recover from the Tampa humidity with their dry cleaning. After a full shift taking shirts and manning the cash register, I'd walk back home to my apartment. I was still living with my mom.

I still remember the first time I saw Armando. At the time, my boyfriend and our group of friends were super into fitness. My boyfriend's twin brother would share Armando's videos online. And the first time I saw Armando was, of course, online. I was scrolling on my Instagram Explore page, when I saw this man lifting a massive weight, in his uniform, and making it look like a piece of cake.

Then, my best friend Jenna shared one of Armando's videos with me online.

"We should totally follow this guy!" She texted and sent a video of one of Armando's fitness challenges.

Jenna wanted to get into shape to join the military, and I wanted to get take my fitness more serious because I was considering being a personal trainer.

I was scrolling through my Instagram when I saw a video Armando had posted on his story asking his audience if they could do something silly with their tongue. Who would have thought that such a random post could bring two people from two different walks of life together for the long haul?

II – ARMANDO

As Navathebeast, I made thousands of posts and heard from people around the world, but only one video brought my future wife into my life.

I'd spend hours editing till the early hours of the morning, painstakingly making sure everything looked slick and professional, but one of the most significant video posts I'd ever made took about twenty seconds to film. I was in my car, and a random idea came to mind. I'd make a quick video asking my audience a question.

Just a quick post to make some small talk with my audience.

"Alright, listen up! Do you know how to do this with your tongue? I cannot do it! If you do, send me a video!"

I scrunched up my face and tried to roll up my tongue for the camera.

Then I posted the video and watched my inbox fill up with random responses from all sorts of people.

Then Pearl's video dropped in my inbox.

I stared at the girl in the video. She looked genuine. And her video made me laugh. I did a quick scan of her social media—she was beautiful, smart, and definitely had a boyfriend. But no matter. I was still in the "I can have whoever

I want" mentality because of my channel. And if I saw that a woman was in a relationship, I looked at her relationship as an extra challenge or hurdle to jump over.

I messaged her.

A few weeks later, we spoke for the first time.

I was traveling for work and was in a hotel. I had brought a woman up to my room, and we had slept together. When the woman left, I had this empty feeling inside. Our time together was never enough or never satisfying.

I started thinking about Pearl, so I called her up on video chat, not fully expecting she'd be awake. It was probably 2 a.m. in the morning, but she was not only awake, she was also making spaghetti. She had just come from a late night at the gym and was making what looked like the worst pot of pasta I'd ever seen. We made each other laugh, and I felt like I was a kid again. It was like I was with my old Runescape girlfriend. I could chat freely about nerdy things and didn't have to put on airs.

III – PEARL

I made a twenty-second video of myself. I had no makeup on, hair all a mess, and pressed send. I honestly didn't think too much about it. Armando was a celebrity and an influencer, so I didn't think of him as a real person. I barely had any followers on my Instagram. I never thought he'd even open up my video.

I was shocked when I checked my inbox. I had a message from THE Armando Nava. What a change of pace from the laundromat. I couldn't believe he liked my video and reached out.

He wrote something flirty, and we started messaging each other back and forth.

After that night when he called, I felt like I was in a romantic-comedy movie.

And like any romantic comedy, a girl has to have a funny best friend. So, I called Jenna and started freaking out.

"You're not going to believe it! Navathebeast responded to my video!"

She was super excited, too. He was a true celebrity.

I thought he was handsome, but I was dating someone else. I told my boyfriend about Armando.

Then Armando invited me to New York!

I had never been to that part of the US. I'd only seen The Big Apple in the movies. So, there was something really exciting and romantic about going to see this larger-than-life guy in the city. I asked Jenna to come with me so we could go meet Navathebeast in person.

I knew what to expect. I'm going to flirt, have a fun time, say goodbye, and go back to the laundromat. But for one weekend, Jenna and I would live out an adventure.

We both wanted something completely different, and bigger. Tampa made me feel boxed in, and so many dark memories were still looming large. The New York invite was perfect.

Jenna and I chatted about what the trip would look like.

"You know he probably does this with a lot of girls," she said.

"I know."

I accepted that this trip would be a quick flash in the pan. In a way, it was easier for me to accept that this wasn't going to be more than a fling since I was still protective of my heart. You can't get hurt if you don't have expectations. I didn't want to give anyone a free pass to hurt me again.

I broke up with my boyfriend, hopped on a plane, and set off to meet my future husband.

Well, first, I wound up getting lost.

I had no idea how to navigate New York. Jenna and I took the wrong train stop and wound up far away from where we were supposed to meet Armando.

IV– ARMANDO

I was still playing by the rulebook for how to pick up a girl that I had learned as a kid, and to that point, I had been pretty successful. I didn't think that night would be any different.

I planned our entire evening. It included tea with my friend Louis. He was in the Marine Corps, and we met in New York. He was a Hispanic Cholo from Texas originally, and we hit it off immediately. New York can swallow a man up—make you forget yourself. But when I was with Louis, it was like I was back home in McAllen. We'd drive around NYC listening to Mexican music on full blast. In Hispanic music, there's something called a *grito*—it's this joyful yell belted out during a song. I can remember many times during a *carne asada* when my *tio* or *tias* would burst into a *grito*—and that's how you knew the party was bumping.

So, naturally, as two dudes in NYC away from our roots, we'd drive around the city, and Louis would belt his *gritos* as loud as he could from the car. It felt like home.

We'd walk around shady areas of New York at all hours of the night—fearless and feeling like gods.

Louis was the best hype-man you could ever ask for. He was my best friend, a handful of years older than me, and already married.

He would make me feel like a god before we'd hit the town, and then when we'd meet up with our dates and he'd hype me up to eleven! "This guy is amazing! Do you know who he is! He's such a good guy!"

The other great thing about having Louis as a buddy, he was always down to strategize. We'd talk about the night ahead of time—going over our plan for how to wine and dine the women, and then when the night was over, we'd debrief about what went well and what we'd do differently next time. We loved having a plan. We loved being in control.

I had cycled through this itinerary so many times. I already knew what I would say to try to make her laugh. Then we'd have a few drinks, and then we'd go to the hookah lounge for karaoke night where we'd play seductive Mexican tunes on the jukebox. Everyone knew us at the lounge. I was a regular.

My drink of choice was Jameson on the rocks. And after a lot of wining and dining, I'd take the woman back to my place. It was a whole production.

The first step was impressing the dates with Navathebeast stuff. In my mind, "Navathebeast" was the reason women flew around the country to meet me. So, they would want to hear about some of the new business plans I had, some of the people I'd met, the places I'd been.

I paused for her reaction.

Nothing.

I glanced over at her.

Nothing.

Usually, the girls I'd meet would be impressed. But nothing was working with this girl.

She did not follow my formula. She wasn't like anyone I had ever met.

V – PEARL

I remember thinking he was so handsome. He was in good shape and wore a button-down shirt. He pulled up in his Chrysler 200 with his friend and when he got out of the car, it was just like a movie. He was handsome, and I couldn't believe this was happening. And then, well, then he opened his mouth.

He began chatting about himself. Nonstop. And within a few minutes of meeting him he was already filming a video.

I thought, This guy's in love with himself. And I figured it was probably because he was around a lot of people hyping him up all the time.

Jenna was eating up everything Armando was saying, I thought, *Girl is this seriously working on you!*

I was so surprised, because over the phone my impression was that he was super down to earth. I was confused. And I thought, Ok I am not going to give this guy the satisfaction of looking impressed.

I also felt pretty small all of a sudden. I hadn't accomplished my dreams and came from a small town in Cuba. I had a hard time connecting with him, or even knowing how to relate. So, within the first few minutes of meeting, I thought *This is a lot of fun, but we are too different.*

Don't get me wrong, a lot of what he said *was* impressive. He had already lived a huge life and had done things I couldn't even imagine. But I didn't say any of that aloud.

The less I cared, the less nervous I became.

The evening progressed, and soon we were in front of the Brooklyn Bridge. We let our friends chat privately because they seemed to be totally hitting it off. We sat down on a little bench and looked at the water.

New York was a lot different from the movies. I remember thinking it was going to be charming and romantic, but there was so much trash on the street. It wasn't what I had expected at all.

And my romantic lead was trying to ask me questions, but I had shut down. I was very short with him and dry. A protective wall went right up, and I thought, I can have fun without getting hurt. I didn't want to flatter him even more or boost that ego.

From there we went to eat at a famous pizza joint. At that point it was obvious we were not vibing at all.

Then we decided to drop by his house and change clothes.

When we got there, I was really surprised by how small the place was. He had told me he lived in a house in New York. So, I thought, *wow, that is impressive,* since the city is so expensive. But when we drove up to the house, I realized it wasn't quite what he had advertised. There was a house, but Armando didn't live in the house, he lived in this little casita behind the house. Like a mother-in-law suite or a little shack. This was THE Nava, and he was living in a little 800-square-foot shack.

He changed his clothes, and I looked around the room.

There were clothes everywhere, a laptop, a bed on the floor. The mattress was disgusting. It was an old and nasty bed. It looked well used.

It was a disaster, and suddenly I saw Armando as a human, not a celebrity.

When he came out of the bathroom, he had changed into a tight yellow shirt with birds on it, and white tight pants.

I whispered a joke to Jenna.

Armando asked me what we were laughing about, and I took a second to respond. I thought he might get offended or even be mad at me if I made a joke at his expense.

I repeated the joke dryly to Armando.

He burst out laughing.

And the air totally cleared. We started cracking jokes back and forth. Both our personalities totally changed. It was like we had disarmed a ticking time bomb with laughter. We defused each other. He showed me a different side of himself—the real Armando Nava. And I kinda liked that guy.

Later that night, his friend said, "He never acts like this," but I wondered if the friend was being a good wingman.

We grabbed margaritas at one of his local stops. And the good times kept rolling.

When I got up to go to the bathroom, Jenna and a girlfriend of Armando's friend joined me. On the way, she said, "Listen, don't get mixed up with Armando. He comes here all the time with different girls. I've seen him buy those margaritas for dozens of girls before you."

I had prepared mentally for this. I had no expectations beyond meeting

Armando. But I could see how girls could get caught up with him and maybe get their hearts broken.

VI – ARMANDO

She wasn't into the persona or the playbook. When you create a personality, you think someone will only want to be with you because of that persona. These girls were not flying to New York to meet me—they were coming to meet "Navathebeast" or the version they saw of me online. I'd chatter about myself because it was easier to keep talking than be quiet and have people see the real me. It helped me stay in control. Be in control of the evening, and not have to fully get to know a woman, to be vulnerable and risk getting hurt emotionally.

But nothing I did worked on Pearl. The longer the night went on, the less we spoke.

It actually became pretty awkward. And I didn't like to waste a good time out. I had been texting another woman earlier in the day. During those days, I was messaging and in contact with several women at the same time. I always kept a backup plan for another girl to hang out with if my date didn't work out. My YouTube pick-up artists had shown me that if one woman doesn't work out, just move on to the next.

I called Louis and told him the date was probably going to be a bust.

Most of the women who would come back to my little shack were already drunk. I didn't care how the place looked because, in my mind, it was only good for one thing: sex. And after we were done, the women would be on their way. It was totally transactional. But when Pearl came back to my place, she wasn't drunk. She was stone-cold sober. Since we weren't gelling, I figured it didn't matter. I'd bring her back so I could change my clothes, and then we'd go out, and I'd probably meet another woman later in the evening.

But after Pearl and I started laughing together, everything changed.

We wound up having a really good time together. And our conversation felt genuine. I hadn't let my guard down like that with a woman in a long, long time. Being with her felt comfortable and easy.

I expected Pearl to pack up her bags and leave forever. But I didn't want her to leave. I didn't understand how to get someone to love me. In my world, I believed I needed to be cruel to women to get them to stay. It was all tricks and reverse psychology. So, the next day when I was driving Pearl back to the train, I decided to stir up some drama.

VII– PEARL

The night before I left for Tampa, he said he'd be interested in pursuing a relationship with me so long as I blocked my ex-boyfriend from my socials.

"Ok, you need to choose right here, right now. Him or me. Delete and block him right now, or this is over," he said.

It might sound strange, but I wasn't annoyed by Armando's ultimatum. I was intrigued. I had never dated a guy who was that assertive. It reminded me of the stories about my Dad. It was a little unsafe.

I deleted the ex and got on the plane back to Florida.

But when I landed in Tampa, Armando said he didn't want to date anymore. This would kick off a pretty emotionally draining pattern of rejection and acceptance.

He didn't want to be with me, but he did. And he would continue texting me or FaceTiming with me every day.

VIII – ARMANDO

The next few days, my friends knew something was up.

"You're not catching feelings, are you?!"

I was. And Pearl and I kept texting. I didn't feel lonely when I was with her. After three months, I felt like I had shown her the real me. And to be honest, that made me uncomfortable.

I always pushed people away when they got too close. The more people would press in, the more I would recoil or want to punish them for daring to get close to me.

I was constantly testing the people around me—trying to see if they really did care for me.

"If you actually like me, you'll book a flight and come here tomorrow," I texted her out of the blue.

"What?" she texted back.

Then I texted: "I saw your ex-boyfriend liked one of your photos on Instagram. I thought you said you blocked him. You lied to me. Have you been with him this whole time?"

"You're going to pay for what you did. Either you come tonight, or we're done."

In hindsight, it is hard to explain. I needed to believe she would do anything for me. I wanted to make sure she was real. She felt too good to be true.

Looking back, I wanted to make myself invincible. If I cared for someone, then they could break my heart or leave me. So, I would hurt them before they could hurt me.

I often thought about getting dropped off at the Walmart parking lot. The feeling of getting kicked out of my mom's car. I avoided commitment with women to avoid experiencing that pain again. Plus, I was used to being alone. It was what I knew.

There was also something a bit darker underneath. Before I met Jesus, I not only wanted to be with many women, I wanted to break them down emotionally. And like I had learned exactly what triggered my mother's pain, I was able to quickly sniff out any weakness and use it against a woman.

I would say whatever I had to say to gain a woman's trust and heart and then leave them. If a girl ever invited me to church with her, I made it my mission to break her faith.

There was one girl who I went on a date with, and she invited me to church. She told me she was saving herself for marriage.

I seduced her and took her virginity. And in my head, I thought, "You see? You see how powerful your God is? He didn't stop you from sleeping with me."

I wanted to be my own God.

When you're a Marine, you learn how to disarm and kill people. How to strategically and efficiently take someone down. I guess you could say, I took the same tactics and applied them to human emotions.

I was very emotionless myself. No crying. I had shut off my emotions. I was robotic. I wouldn't want to hug or hold hands or do anything overly affectionate. Our family wasn't overly lovey with each other, and then the military amplified those feelings.

Pearl flew back to New York the next day and passed my test.

I invited her to come live nearby in San Antonio.

IX – PEARL

I needed to get out of Florida, and I was in love. So, I moved to San Antonio with Jenna to be near Armando. Jenna and I got a little apartment. I still remember feeling amazed by how big it was compared to our home in Tampa.

I thought Armando and I were going to be together all the time. But it wasn't what I expected.

We had the same humor. I was a female version of him. To this day, we are very similar. From music, movies, videos, family, humor, we just had a lot in common and felt like we could be silly with each other. And that was the difference. Suddenly he wasn't trying to impress me or impress his audience on social media. He was being himself.

I've never laughed with somebody like we laughed together in those early days. You know, where your stomach hurts so bad because you've laughed so hard. It was an incredible change to be around someone with whom I could cut up and let go. Making him laugh was amazing.

The timing of my move to Texas was perfect. It allowed me to get out of Tampa to make a life for myself somewhere different. In a way, to start over.

The exact path for my future wasn't clear. But I was ready for some movement, ready to take a risk.

I saw Armando as someone offering me an invitation for a bigger life, and I took it. I thought, Even if it doesn't work out, at least I'm out of Tampa, at least I've made a change, I'm doing something different.

The biggest hurdle I had to face was my mom. Being her only child—and the only family she had in the USA—I thought she would take it pretty hard. But mom had followed her own dreams, and it's because of her dreams that we left Cuba. I think, on some level, she understood me better than I realized. She could see that I was going for a bigger life, just like she had so many years earlier.

When I moved to San Antonio, I wasn't a Christian. And I didn't know that I was moving into a ticking time bomb. Armando was just about to transition out of the military and enter a dark night of the soul.

X – ARMANDO

In August 2019, I was officially out of the uniform. And I didn't know what I was going to do with my life. People wanted to see my Marine content. I had built this whole persona over being the guy who shows you behind the scenes in the military. I wasn't sure who I was without the Marines. I felt like I couldn't please my audience. They wanted "Navathebeast" content, but I wasn't in the military anymore.

Plus, everything I did online was being scrutinized. Memes, horrible comments, people judging me for *leaving* the military. When I was in the military, I didn't care if people judged me. It was like I was making content for a bigger purpose—if they didn't like my content, it didn't feel personal. Outside of the military, I had time to read comments; it really messed with my head. I started listening to the haters. I was so sucked into the negative feedback that I literally didn't want to live.

I lost my superpower, which was the uniform. It was my purpose and shield. I felt like being a Marine was the best part of being me. And I wasn't anything without it. Once again, I was that kid in the gaming utility closet—just a regular person. A nobody. A Texas nobody.

That's when I started to drink heavily.

I was excited about Pearl moving out, but as soon as she landed in San Antonio, I started resenting her. With her in San Antonio, I didn't feel comfortable seeing other women. Seeing her was a reminder that I needed to settle down. But I wasn't ready to let go of that lifestyle. So, I held her at a distance. I kept our relationship private. No online mentions of a girlfriend meant I could still be a player. I didn't want to squash my chances with other women.

My family thought we were making a mistake. What if y'all break up, and she's moved all the way out here?

So, I started to act out, to take my anger out on Pearl. I'd tell her not to come over, that I needed some space.

Between August and November 2019, I started taking classes to pass the real estate exam to get my license. On my first day of real estate class, I ambled into class without my books and a mouth full of dip. I sat at the back and popped open a Monster energy drink. As I stretched back in my chair like a recliner, I eyed the teacher, thinking to myself, *This scene is not for me.*

As the teacher droned on, I started zoning out and decided that this was a waste of time. By the middle of the day, I decided to leave.

Not surprisingly, I failed the real estate test.

And then I failed again.

And again.

AND again.

I failed the test five times before passing it. School and the framework of the classroom were so uncomfortable that I decided I would learn from memorizing what was on the test and learn from my mistakes.

Pearl, being a naturally good student, would encourage me to study—like a normal person. But every time I opened my books, I felt overwhelmed. So, I tackled the test my way.

I'd drive hours to different cities in Texas to take the exam at different locations. Each time I'd do a little better, until I finally passed the test. I was so desperate to prove that I could make something of my life outside of the military.

And, of course, I filmed this whole process—still puffing myself up online. The hard thing about having thousands of followers is that you have to give them a reason to show up to your channel day after day. At the time, I felt like I needed to give them a show. I needed my audience to think I was crushing it outside the military. I was determined to not be another depressed veteran struggling with who they are outside of the uniform. But I was depressed, and nothing was working.

That's when those old demons came back, and they brought friends. Those voices who had whispered in my ear since I was a child—*Loser, you're nothing, life isn't worth living*—turned up the volume.

After finally passing the real estate exam, I started working with my brother selling apartments. He had hyped me to his boss and colleagues, totally vouched for me. But I quit after one month. Office life was too boring and monotonous. *I'm not a real estate guy. I am a social media dude, I thought.*

My backup backup plan wasn't even working out. Real estate was our family business, and I felt like I'd failed everything. I started spiraling. I was depressed. I didn't want to call people, I didn't want to talk to people.

Meantime, I was toying with the idea of going back into the military.

It was about a month after I left the Marines, and I got a call from a sergeant.

I was really struggling when I took the phone call. Nothing was working out career-wise, and I was totally inside my head, drinking too much and reading online hate around the clock.

One of my friends, a Gunnery Sergeant, who was in his thirties called me up one day. We partied together and had many conversations about the future.

The Gunnery sergeant said he could bring me back to California, and my Navathebeast channel could really explode again. I'd have more money, more viewers, and more opportunities than ever before.

The thing was... Pearl.

I had just brought her out to San Antonio, and I was committed to starting a civilian life.

I told this to the Sergeant, and that's when the tone of his voice changed.

"You're an absolute idiot. Forget the girl. Get out here. There's nothing for you where you're at," he said forcefully.

In the back of my mind, there was a quiet voice that said simply, "Wait. There's something better for you if you can just wait."

I hung up the phone and began pacing back and forth on my balcony while mainlining tequila.

As the tequila set in, and my mind went cloudy, everything hit me all at once. All the comments online, all the memes and hate, all my failed businesses, feeling like a disappointment to my family—all the voices came flooding over me. I took another shot of tequila to tamp them down, but it just turned up the volume.

I had been angry for so many years of my life, but in that moment, I felt an overwhelming feeling of grief.

With a glass of tequila in my hand, I looked over the balcony. The ground didn't seem so far away.

The voices nudged me nearer to the edge, and I put my leg on the other side of the balcony and closed my eyes.

I couldn't go back to the military, but I couldn't stay where I was anymore. I was so exhausted and so aimless. For a moment, I thought, maybe I should end it all.

But that other voice—the quieter voice I had heard on the phone earlier, began getting louder: "Wait. Be patient. I have good things in store for you."

I climbed back over the rail shivering and sweating before coming to my senses.

I'm going to stay put. This isn't finished. I thought to myself.

I was in the car with my mother and Pearl when the Sergeant called again.

"So, when are we signing you back up?" he asked.

"It's not happening," I said. "I'm going to stay here."

He started cussing me out on the phone. It was such a strong reaction that I hung up on him and blocked his number.

I felt immediate relief after the phone call ended, knowing I had passed some sort of test and could fully commit to the adventure at hand.

Most days, I battled my demons. I was alone in this apartment, and it reminded me of my lonely formative years. When it came to my channel, I felt like I was trying to rub two sticks together to make a fire.

I hated the nighttime; that's when the voices of doubt would overpower me.

I hated the person I saw in the mirror.

But when the camera was rolling, I was back to "beast mode" and cheesing. I never wanted people to know how much I was struggling.

"What's up guys! I've had a great day! So excited about some new developments! I'll keep ya'll updated!" I'd say while smiling at the camera.

As soon as I put the phone away, I would collapse into the couch with a glass of tequila and wonder what I was going to do with my life.

Before leaving the military, I had started a supplement company. I was able to get sponsored by brand companies and make commissions off sales. I thought I *could make more if I just created my own thing.* I'd highlight the effects of my supplements in my videos. I started taking off, and I had to hire people. *I'm turning a corner,* I thought. It was going really well until it wasn't.

I didn't know how to run a company. I was just winging it. And unfortunately, someone I hired ended up stealing from my company and me. That discouraged me. When my colleague stole money, it confirmed my fear. I had taken a risk and relied on someone other than myself. *Never again,* I thought. *Better to be a lone wolf and in control than be taken advantage of.* I shut the whole supplement company down shortly after that.

I couldn't make military content outside the service, nor could I make money off supplements. I was doubly disappointed.

That's when I started to train people online. I'm like, *Okay I gotta pivot. I'm going to be an online trainer. I'm gonna be fit, get super swole, and do my videos.*

I knew some of the fitness influencers—met them at a few parties. In fact, I had a chance to meet one of the guys I used to watch online as a kid. He was one of my inspirations. I couldn't believe I was in the same room as him. He had been my idol.

But my online classes weren't selling, and the hate was at an all-time high.

And I lashed out at the one person who loved me no matter what. Pearl had only been in San Antonio for a few months when I told her I didn't think our relationship was going to work out. "I have too much in my mind," I said, "I need to focus on my career." I was cold and cruel.

And she was heartbroken but not angry. Instead of blaming, she asked how she could help me. I was shocked. The more I pulled away, the more she leaned in—she wasn't afraid or ashamed of me. She wanted to help me. But I couldn't see past my failure—so I continued with the on again/off again cycle for weeks—breaking up in dramatic ways, getting back together, etc. Until finally I told her I was going to buy her a ticket back to Tampa.

CHAPTER 7

San Antonio

Be kind to one another, tenderhearted, forgiving one another, as God in Christ forgave you.

—EPHESIANS 4:32

I – PEARL

It has taken me many years to be open about this time in my life. As a child of abuse, there's a lot of pain you cannot control. You'd think that once I became an adult, when sensing another abusive situation, I'd run for the hills. But that's not how these things work.

I knew Armando was the kind of man I couldn't keep a tight grip on. I remembered how my grandmother tried to keep my grandfather on a leash, and how that never worked for them. I remembered the woman in the teal house in Cuba.

With my move to San Antonio, I decided it was going to make it my job to love this man.

I didn't own a car, so Armando connected me with his mother, Maria, so I could babysit her daughter, Franchesca. It was a fun job, and I loved getting to know Armando's family. But I didn't realize what I was walking into. By the time I arrived in San Antonio, Armando was only a few weeks out of his military service. I knew he was struggling, but he was guarded and didn't want to share his pain.

We started our relationship in a strange cloud of dysfunction. He was my boyfriend, and he was my entire world. But it felt like the closer I got to him, the more he disliked me.

Looking back, I wonder if it was a survival tactic. He would try to hide who he was from everyone. But I could see the man behind the camera. And, although I wasn't sure what I was going to do with my life, I knew that this man was going to impact the world, and I wanted to be with him no matter the cost.

After my babysitting job, I'd go visit Armando. He was living with his brother, and those first few weeks, we had a blast—there was a lot of drinking and overall, we had fun being together. But we couldn't camouflage our pain indefinitely.

Then out of the blue, Armando said he didn't want to see me. We were still together, but I had the sense he wanted to date other people.

Many women might have left, but I was a perfect target, used to taking things silently for many years, all in stride, I couldn't picture my life without this man. So, even after our relationship turned toxic, I stayed.

All those creeping insecurities I had harbored since I was a child—that I had no purpose to live outside of a relationship—began flooding back inside of me.

I'd try to give Armando space, but he wanted to know where I was at all times. He'd be furious with me for hanging out with my friend, but equally angry with me for being around him. His behavior became super controlling and possessive.

I was desperate to please him. I didn't want to lose him. And I wanted him to love me.

He'd start testing me again. I could tell he wanted me to prove my love for him. I could tell he wanted to see how far he could push me before I left. So, he made me do strange things, like go wait for him outside his house in the Texas heat. For hours.

It was controlling. And it was the pattern for several months. Push and pull. I want you, I hate you.

And slowly, the confidence that I had worked so hard to build up through-out my senior year of high school and years in college began to erode. I was drained. I felt like I couldn't do anything right. I was happy to have a man like Armando, but my entire world revolved around him.

Then he began saying cruel things to me, like, "You're not contributing anything; you're worthless."

I would think, *Ok, I need to go get a job to prove my worth.*

One day I had an interview lined up for a job, and he wouldn't let me go. He was going to drive me there and decided not to. It was a control move.

He said, "No, no I don't want you to work there."

That fall in 2019, we broke up and got back together again and again. I started losing weight because I was in a constant state of stress.

I didn't share anything with my mom or friends during that period, I didn't want them to worry. I'd tell them that things between Armando and me were good. If Mom knew about the emotional manipulation I was going through, she would have told me to pack up my bags and leave.

I did what I had done since I was a child. I turned all my secrets over to my prayer journal, and I began asking God to save me.

I wouldn't say I was a true follower of Christ at that time in my life, but I under-stood enough to believe there was something bigger out there, something or some-one who cared about my life. That fall, I began writing letters to my father again.

I began developing a relationship with God from a place of survival, and reading scripture was healing to my soul.

Dear Dad,

I've learned so much from Armando, especially about talking to people. Even though I still get anxious, I've seen how similar you both are. I wish you could have met him. The conversations between the two of you would have been epic—two great minds sharing thoughts.

Thank you for watching over me, Dad. I know you're around. I have felt you a couple of times. When A and I broke up, I felt you sitting next to me at church. You and God never left my side, and for that, I am eternally grateful. I love you, Dad. I'll talk to you soon, I promise, but I need to finish up some laundry. I'll keep writing. I have a new journal with empty pages waiting to be filled. So, it gives me an excuse to write. Lol.

Love, your daughter.

Hey Dad

It's been a while since I've written. I think about a month or two if I'm not mistaken. There have been some ups and downs that I'm sure you're aware of. Things are smoother, and they seem to be falling into place. Dad, I know you can see Mom, and I wanted to ask you to take care of her. Please stay close to her. Please bring her closer to God. God is coming soon, and I don't want her to go somewhere she doesn't belong. Dad, I always wonder if you're in heaven. I read somewhere that said that we would reunite with our loved ones up there. I hope you are because I would love to meet you. Anyways, A and I are really good. We are working as a team. We are trying to make our dreams come true. I feel deeper in love with him as the days pass.

We are so similar yet so different; it's just weird to meet a soul so similar to yours that has been molded by a different path. Now we are on the same path. God brought us together to fulfill His purpose.

One night, it was probably 3 a.m. in the morning, Armando shook me awake from a deep sleep.

"Hey! What are you doing with your life?" he said as he shook me.

"Like, what do you mean?" I asked sleepily and confused, "I'm working. What do you want from me?" I pleaded.

We spent the rest of the night arguing.

That became a normal occurrence.

It was difficult mentally. I could tell he was trying to get rid of me. But at the same time, I didn't believe he wanted to really leave me. I could see the real him—someone who had been hurt. I took the brunt of his anger. And I tried to redirect his frustrations as best as I could. But loving him was a challenge. My own insecurities of not being good enough, or being weird, or not being worth loving, started to haunt me.

It all came to a head on New Year's 2019.

On December 30, Armando came to my apartment. I knew by the look on his face something was wrong.

"I bought you a plane ticket, and you're gonna pack up all your stuff, and you're gonna leave. I can't do a relationship right now," he said.

And I pushed back. "I live here now. My life is here, with or without you. Even if we break up, I'm going to stay here," I said.

I begged him not to leave me.

I was crying and wailing, and after I thought I didn't have any more to give, he said randomly, "Let's go get pancakes."

I thought, *Ok so you're going to shatter my heart and then eat in front of me.*

When he dropped me back at my apartment, my heart was completely shattered. A belly full of gross pancakes and tears.

Jenna had gone to Tampa for the holidays. I was alone in the apartment, and that's when it hit me—he was serious. We were really breaking up. The walls started to close in around me. All those old lies the enemy had been whispering in my ear since I was a child started shouting.

I went into Jenna's medicine cabinet and took a fistful of her pain pills. I wrote a suicide letter apologizing to everyone in my family.

And I laid down to die.

II – ARMANDO

Our story isn't a fairytale. I can admit now, as a changed man, that I was verbally abusive.

I would test Pearl in extreme ways. I wanted to see how far she would go to love me, and I would humiliate her. I know it sounds strange—how can you love someone and want to hurt them? But I was trapped by my god-mindset ego. Wanting someone to fully and totally submit to me, I put all of the tactics I had learned over the years from YouTube into practice.

I would purposefully put Pearl through tests. I'd lock her out of my house. I'd push her away. I'd yell at her. I expected her to leave, but she didn't. And the longer she stayed, the angrier it made me.

I was the one who invited her to come to San Antonio, but once she was there, I couldn't hide. I invited her into my own space and couldn't handle that level of intimacy. I took it out on here, I tried to destroy her. This gift that God had given me, this beautiful person inside and out I was ready to completely crush her.

Still trying to figure out my career post-military, most days were spent spinning my wheels, throwing stuff at the wall to see what would stick. I didn't want anyone to see me in that vulnerable state—especially someone who had moved to Texas to be with THE Navathebeast.

I didn't feel like a beast at all. I was becoming more and more depressed—not knowing how to deal with my emotions and with the onslaught of negative social media posts. So, I lashed out at this beautiful person who loved me. What would she think if she really knew the guy she had moved across the country for was a regular nobody?

I picked her apart again and again: "What are you doing here? Why are you here?"

"I live here. You asked me here." She'd calmly respond.

And I'd say cruel things. "You don't do anything. You have nothing in your life."

I'd test her with scenarios I had learned in the military. "Pack up your bed. Pack up your bags. Get out of here." When she was busy gathering her belongings, I'd say, "Put it back. Put it all back."

I wanted to break her down the way I had been broken down. But she didn't leave. I was shocked. Why is she still here?

I'd call her words like worthless and pathetic. *You don't have a job; you're only good for sex.* I was begging her to leave. But the meaner I became, the more she pressed in.

I didn't know at first that she was praying for me.

It wasn't until I found one of her letters that I realized she had been taking out her frustrations in a prayer journal.

I read.

I took her journal and ripped out some of her letters.

"These letters aren't going to change anything!" I yelled at her. "Quit praying for me. Don't waste your time. Get a job. God is not here," I said and stormed off to the gym.

She was quiet. Then she gathered up the torn letters and put them back in her journal. When I came back home, it was like nothing had changed. She was still writing in her journal and still reading the Bible like nothing had happened.

I took the book out of her hand and threw it against the wall.

I had no interest in her letters or the God she was writing to.

After that, she'd try to tell me about things she was learning through the scriptures, but when she'd bring up the topic, it would make me see red.

Pearl didn't fight back or get angry when I criticized her new faith. I had never been around a human like this before. It was weird.

She was learning about Christ's unconditional love and trying to love me at my worst. I couldn't comprehend it. I hadn't grown up with that kind of love. I couldn't believe it was real, let alone that there was an all-loving Creator of the Universe. It was too hard to believe. But it was real. Pearl's love was real, and it scared me. How could I trust it?

One day she was reading her Bible, and I grabbed it from her hands. *I'm going to try to disprove this junk*, I thought.

And that was the first time I started reading the Bible. I can't say there was an immediate impact—but like the Parable of the Sower says in Matthew, seeds were planted.

I wasn't ready to risk giving up the life I knew for the terrible vulnerability required in the life Pearl was growing in daily. I wasn't ready to give up being in control, being my own god. So, I put the Bible away and continued to try to build up another empire by myself.

And my first order of business was getting rid of the woman who was convicting me with love.

On December 30, I woke up thinking about what the following year would bring. New business? New career? New relationships? I wasn't sure how to visualize 2020, but I knew I needed to start over and feel totally free. So, I drove over to Pearl's apartment to break up with her, to be done with her once and for all.

I bought her a ticket to Tampa and tried to force her to leave. But she wasn't leaving.

"Fine, if you won't leave, I will," I said before I hopped in my car and drove to McAllen. My plan was to surprise my Dad for New Year's Eve and hang out downtown with some of my old buddies.

I made the four-hour drive from San Antonio to McAllen when I got a text from my mom.

"Have you checked on Pearl?"

"No," I texted, thinking about her tear-stained face. "I broke up with her," I texted my Mom.

Mom was always understanding. We texted back and forth, and then she finally said, "I'm going to invite her to our New Year's party."

"No problem," I texted.

I pulled into my Dad's driveway. My uncle opened the door and said Dad was out back grilling. Of course. The King of the *Carne Asada* was at his post again.

Then I had the weirdest sensation come over me. I needed to get back to San Antonio ASAP. Something was not right.

I didn't even take a step inside my father's house. I turned around and got back in the car, speeding all the way back to San Antonio.

When I arrived, my family was in good spirits celebrating the holiday.

"Where's Pearl," I asked my Mom.

She was in the bedroom lying down.

I had taken down all the pictures of us off my walls. I found her exhausted and tear-stained on my bed.

As the New Year's countdown played on the TV, we could hear fireworks. We didn't have a heart-to-heart. We didn't talk about what had happened. I didn't say anything. I just hugged her.

Everyone left, and we ended up spending the night there. I didn't want her to leave. But I didn't know what I wanted at that point.

In the middle of the night, Pearl began violently throwing up. She told me she must have eaten something bad, and I believed her.

I was worried. As she emptied so much of her stomach, nothing was coming up anymore. I drove her to an emergency room.

When we arrived, the doctors were making a big scene. And I was so confused, thinking, *Man, this is just food poisoning. She probably just needs some fluids.* But they said she needed to stay, or she could die. I thought they were taking advantage of her, trying to make a dime off a sick girl. I had no idea they were pumping her stomach for pills which could have ended her life.

She was in the hospital for two days.

And when she came out of the hospital, we got back together.

We took a trip together the next week, and we had a good time. But as soon as we got back to San Antonio, all of the worries and insecurities I had about my future came flooding back.

I broke up with her again. I knew I was putting her through hell, but I had no idea I had pushed her to the brink of taking her life.

In January 2020, I told Pearl I had no feelings for her. But we didn't end our relationship poorly. I loved her. I didn't know how to commit to her, though.

A few days after our breakup, I found a note Pearl had written to me.

Thank you for last night and everything.
Take care and don't be a stranger.
God has a plan.
P.S call champions.

> *Pearl*

It made me fall in love with her again. This girl had not left me when I had been so cruel. I had pushed her to the brink—and for some reason, she was still here.

I couldn't comprehend this kind of selfless love.

III – PEARL

They pumped my stomach. For the third time in my life, I survived a suicide attempt. I didn't want Armando to know what I had done.

I was not expecting to wake up in 2020. But life kept moving forward. At the hospital, I emptied everything out of my body. Literally everything. I had nothing left in my body or soul.

It was like I had received a gift from God to continue living. When I got up out of the hospital bed, I was even more resolute in loving this man who had hurt me.

But this time, I would love him through my life and not my death.

Armando's mom understood what I was going through, and although she was always fiercely loyal to her son, I could tell that her heart broke for us. She had been on the receiving end of Armando's anger, and we could relate to each other.

I felt totally numb when he broke up with me again in January. And when I came back to my apartment, Jenna wanted to have an intervention.

"This guy is playing with your emotions. I've held my tongue for too long, but I can't stand seeing you like this," she said angrily.

Any friend would react this way, but I had no way to explain to her why I felt so strongly about staying in the relationship.

Jenna encouraged me to break off all contact with Armando and try to move on with my life. I wasn't making enough money to pay my end of the rent, so we were getting evicted and needed to plan our next steps.

My buddy, who was usually so full of energy and always laughing, had finally had enough when she caught me texting Armando.

I had never seen her that mad.

"I'm done listening to you cry. You need to grow up and get over this guy!" she said.

At that point Jenna was taking care of most of our household bills. Armando's Mom was my employer but would often pay me late so I wasn't able to support myself.

What I didn't realize at the time was that my mother had spoken to Jenna about Armando. Jenna knew my mom would be furious with the way I had been treated.

Mom called me with concern, and that made me see red. I was so private and didn't ever want to give my Mom a reason to worry about me, so when I found out Jenna had shared my business to my mother, I was livid.

"I cannot believe you told MY mom MY business. What gives you the right?!" I shouted at Jenna.

"Someone has to speak up for you! You can't keep going on like this," Jenna yelled back at me.

The argument grew more heated and nearly became physical. We were like sisters, and loved each other deeply, so we fought hard.

She was worried about my relationship with Armando, and I couldn't stop loving him.

After we said our peace, we just sat quietly staring at the TV and then eventually hugged each other and cried.

"I think we need to part ways," I said.

Jenna agreed.

Later that same day I went out to dinner with Armando. We hadn't seen each other in weeks. That dinner felt like the first night we were together in New York. The laughing, the humor, the connection. It all came back.

I stuck a simple note to his bathroom mirror and didn't expect to hear from him for a while.

But by the time I got back to my apartment I received a text.

"I want you to move in with me in January," he wrote.

I looked at the words on my phone screen. And I decided to say yes.

CHAPTER 8

Secret Marriage

If we confess our sins, he is faithful and just to forgive us our sins and to cleanse us from all unrighteousness.

—1 JOHN 1:9

I – PEARL

It wasn't a fairytale. It was a secret.

I moved in with Armando in January 2020, and we got married on the 18th of February.

Two broken people trying to build a life together. We had both witnessed our parents use marriage as a fix-all. And I thought, *If he marries me, then he definitely won't leave me.*

In the weeks before we were married, I was diving into scripture. The Bible was like a life preserver, and I was clinging to it with dear life. I started addressing my letters to Jesus instead of my father. The more I learned about my heavenly Father, the more I realized I was serving a living God.

Dear God,

I read letters I wrote to my "dad" and realized how little knowledge I had. I used to think my birth dad was watching over my mom and me when, in reality, that just isn't true. I gave so much credit to someone who couldn't even lift a finger instead of the one who desires all my praise. You really answered all my past prayers—even ones that I had a difficult time believing. But it takes patience, and I believe you are changing our hearts. It's a work in progress but thank you, God, for teaching me patience and for finding favor in us and guiding us. Whoever winds up reading this, I want you to know that God has not forgotten you. Pray and be patient. Watch how the Lord will transform you.

Thank you, Yeshua

I would turn on worship songs and leave encouraging notes all over the house. I'd gently share what I was learning, but I knew not to pressure Armando into reading the Bible.

Armando didn't want me to go to church because he still wanted to control me. But one weekend, out of the blue, he said was open to going to a service.

We settled on a Seventh Day Adventist church because it was open on Saturday.

My family back in Cuba prayed to the saints, but I never saw examples of what a spirit-filled life could look like. In Cuba, there is a lot of superstition, magic, and voodoo. I always believed there was a bigger energy or something out there, but I didn't know Jesus Christ.

We walked into the small church and sat on the fourth row close to the front of the altar. I remember loving the music, and the congregants passed out tambourines and drums for us to use during worship. Armando fidgeted in his seat, but I was happy he was there.

The pastor gave a sermon about holiness and sin. He mentioned how unmarried people living together were in sin. After the service, an elder invited us to his home for a Bible study.

I wasn't sure what Armando was thinking, but I could see the wheels turning in his mind on the drive home. He started worrying about hell.

The next day, he asked me to marry him.

I was excited and nervous. I was kind of holding my breath the entire time. I didn't want to say something to make him change his mind. I was blindly in love with him, and I felt so small about myself. When he popped the question, I was shocked and said yes immediately.

We went to the courthouse, and I couldn't believe it was happening. But we didn't tell anyone. Nobody knew. We planned to keep it a secret. At that point, we had only been together seven months, so we thought our family would try to talk us out of marriage.

People thought I was his girlfriend.

I hoped things would change once I became his wife. But those first few weeks were some of our most difficult days together.

His cycles of verbal abuse continued. He'd throw all my things on the floor and tell me to leave. I'd pack my belongings in a suitcase while he verbally bombed me. *Do you really want to leave me? Ok, do you really want to be with me?*

Yes, I'd say, *of course.*

Then go ahead and put your stuff away, he'd say.

He could have told me to go out and streak naked, and I would have probably done it. He was never physically violent, but he made me feel ashamed of myself, like I was a helpless kid.

If people knew I was letting someone treat me like this, they would look down and judge me. So, just like our marriage, I kept the abuse a secret.

I was good at keeping the abuse a secret.

Although I was in a difficult situation with my husband, I believed he would change if he could just let this love of the Lord into his heart. I spent forty days reading the entire Bible. At that point, my faith was survival. I'd talk to Jesus about my marriage and about my pain and loneliness. I went to a few Bible studies through the church and shared a little bit about my story with the pastor. He encouraged me to pray for Armando.

Dear God,

Sometimes I wonder if this is the man you gifted me. Is this how it's going to be for the rest of our lives, or will he love me the way you loved the church? I'm not a perfect wife. I make mistakes, but I don't treat him like that when he upsets me. I know that's what the enemy wants; that's why I just take it, but when is it going to stop? There's only so much I can take. I love him and don't want to leave, but he underestimates how much he's actually hurting me.

Armando was open to reading books for self-improvement. So, we went to a bookstore and bought him a Bible. At the time, it was just another book in a stack of his self-improvement books. But, of course, I was praying God would speak to him directly through the Word.

Sometimes he would rip my letters. But I knew he couldn't rip my messages. Everything I wrote, I had already prayed directly to the Lord. Even if the papers were ripped up, I believed the messages were still reaching the Lord. So, I kept writing and kept on praying. And then something precious happened. I started to feel a warm overwhelming love come over me.

For the first time in my life, I started to feel the real love of a father. And the feeling was completely transformative. All at once, I felt God was my protector, my Father, my source of joy and strength. It started with Love.

Dear God,

I already spoke to you in the car, but I just need to write in order to get my feelings out... A said something that really had me thinking. It's not because he hadn't said it before, because he has, but getting closer to you has opened my eyes and you have given me the knowledge to see things as they are. "It's not all about love" were the words that came out of his mouth, the thing is, it is all about love because you are love. In your book, 1 John 4:8 tells us "God is love." John 3:16: "For God so loved the world that he gave his only begotten son, that whosoever believeth in him should not perish, but have everlasting life." Romans 5:8 also states, "But God commendeth his love towards us, in that while we were yet sinners, Christ died for us."

These verses show that everything you did for us was out of love. You don't say "As soon as you clean up your act, I'll love you". You don't love us because we're lovable or because we make you feel good. You love us because you are love. Your love for us is so unconditional that you sent your own son Jesus Christ to die for us while we were still unlovable sinners. So, yes, it is all about love because without it we wouldn't be here.

II – ARMANDO

From a place of fear and chaos, I asked Pearl to be my wife. One week later, I began looking into how to get a divorce. The closer she drew to me, the more I wanted her to get away from me.

I didn't let her tell anyone about our marriage, and I didn't announce anything online. If I posted anything about Pearl, then I would have to end things with the other women I was still flirting with through social media. I wasn't ready to give up the false sense of control that life afforded me.

I took advantage of her love. I viewed her faithfulness as stupidity. I'd demean her and make fun of her for staying with me. *How could you stay with someone who hates you?*

We moved into a house my mom owned in Corpus. And when the pandemic shut down businesses and life as we knew it in early 2020, Pearl and I were stuck together binge-watching TV shows and eating fast food.

At that point, my YouTube channels weren't gaining new subscribers. My whole identity had been tied up in Navathebeast—the personality I'd hid behind in the military. Now out of the military this personality was failing me. Subscriptions had stopped, and Pearl had a front-row seat to my breakdown. And I resented her for it.

After months of hustling and out of ideas I was exhausted and decided to re-enlist in the military.

During that time, I had a conversation with my brother. Sometimes you need an older sibling to kick your butt into gear.

I thought he'd be stoked about me joining the military again, but he stopped me in my tracks.

"Take a look at yourself. You can't even commit to our family business, bro. I gift-wrapped this job for you, and you blew it," he said. "What makes you think you're going to kill it in the military if you can't even commit to a job I gift-wrapped for you?"

My heart wasn't in it, and I wasn't motivated. Still, his words had a profound impact on me. He was right. I hadn't finished what I started. And I needed a challenge.

I slammed the phone down and stormed into the living room.

"Pearl, you're not going to believe what my brother said," and I recounted the conversation.

She listened intently, and we decided to pack up our stuff and finish what I started with my brother in San Antonio.

I promised myself that I would have a life outside of the military. And like I told Roy when I was in high school, I knew I wanted to be in real estate. It was time to buckle down and focus.

What I didn't know was that Pearl was praying for me around the clock, that the Holy Spirit was guiding our steps.

In the spring of 2020, I dove into books about business, and I started focusing on my physical health again.

The second time I showed up at my brother's leasing agency, I arrived correctly. I had monthly goals and threw myself into selling as many apartments as possible to hit my target.

In a matter of months, I wound up becoming the top agent in the office.

I still remember unwrapping the "BEST SALES OF MONTH" plaque with my name on it. It felt good to see my name on the award. It gave me the boost of confidence I needed to continue working in this field. I needed a win. I realized by spending years watching my parents hustle in real estate, I came by the skills of a realtor honestly. Years of watching my parents hustle in this industry, paired with my personality, equipped me to do this job. I was built for the business. I started to feel less depressed and like I could see a way forward again.

As I was ascending in my career, my home life was a mess.

I took Pearl and our marriage for granted. While I was closing deals all day at work, Pearl was taking an online class for me at home. I never wore my wedding ring, and our marriage was still a secret. I slid right back into my Navathebeast habits, talking to girls online and flirting with women in the office. I treated my wife like a maid. She was taking care of my house and doing my schoolwork. I kept a roof over her head and food on her table, but I didn't give myself to her. I still held her at such a distance. We were essentially roommates.

What's worse, as I became more successful with real estate, I came into contact with more women. I'd spend whole days with them before heading back home to my wife. I was bored. I didn't see Pearl as a gift or a prize; I saw her as someone who was holding me back from a life of excitement. I'd resort to my bullying habits. I'd pick fights with her, hoping she would leave me.

III – PEARL

I got in the passenger side of our car, and his wedding ring was in the cup holder. My heart sank. In my core, I knew he was slipping back into his old ways. Just like my mom's marriage to Jose didn't change anything, I started to realize the marriage hadn't changed anything because we hadn't been changed by the Holy Spirit. We were the same broken people trying to make a broken marriage work.

I could feel his energy and knew he wasn't happy. This was so *not* how I had dreamed of my fairytale wedding and marriage.

I wasn't an idiot. I asked Armando why he didn't wear his wedding ring. He said it felt uncomfortable on his finger.

I had a feeling he was seeing someone else. He denied it. Told me there was something wrong with me, and that I was being paranoid.

I knew he was lying when he wanted us to move into a specific apartment building where a woman he was flirty with lived. I remember him selling me on the idea, and I thought *this is just a way for him to have access to this woman and me at the same time.* She was his work wife in a way.

I felt powerless. No one should have to endure this kind of behavior. But the honest truth is I didn't want to lose him. I was so in love with him, and it was easier to look the other way than admit that there was something wrong.

Looking back, that kind of response is pretty typical for survivors of abuse. It's hard to know your worth when you've been treated as subhuman and used for your body alone, never cherished or loved fully. I didn't love myself either, so I allowed myself to be debased thinking, *This is the best I could ever get.*

It wasn't until I started learning about the perfect love of Jesus Christ, who literally gave His life so that I may live, that I started to see myself as a daughter of a King. This revelation was so much better than any Cinderella fairytale I could have ever imagined!

My boyfriends had become my sole reason for living because I didn't see myself as having anything worth living for. But when I read scripture and discovered the love of my heavenly Father, I began to learn more about the Lord and see myself the way He sees me. It was such a huge transformation. I learned the Creator of the Universe values me and my gifts and has created me for "Such a time as this," as is written in the Book of Esther.

And the more I read scripture and discovered God's love, I saw a different future. I wanted to share it with Armando. Instead of nagging or berating him, I continued to write letters to Jesus, begging the Lord to save our marriage and save my husband. I was always super vague with my family. Never oversharing what was really happening. Only our moms knew we were married; everyone else thought we were just boyfriend and girlfriend.

In a way, our marriage was like something out of the 1950s. I made his food and cleaned his house. Dinner was always heated up and on the table by the time he got home. When his sales started taking off, we took a vacation from time to time. But there was certainly a cost. I didn't feel safe emotionally. I wasn't sure what kind of man was going to walk through the doors.

I'd keep the house immaculate and do everything to the best of my abilities, but he'd find some way to break me down.

Those were hard times, but I am glad to tell you that God had a bigger plan for our marriage.

I began studying to get a real estate license, so I could help support Armando.

One day while I was studying, Armando took my real estate study book, and ripped off the cover.

I kept holding onto hope for him because I knew once the message of Jesus Christ got ahold of Armando, not only would our marriage be saved, but hundreds of people could be touched.

As a wife, I saw my role as a supporter and encourager. I could also see Armando as God saw him and knew he had the potential to really touch people's lives.

I knew that our marriage wasn't going to survive without the Grace of God. I also knew my husband wasn't interested in learning about this living God whom I had encountered. But he was interested in success, so we talked about Proverbs. He started reading them. And I saw him soften a little.

I realized that the way Armando was treating me had more to do with what was going on inside of him, and if I really wanted my marriage to survive, he was going to have an encounter with the Holy Spirit.

I kept writing all my fears and worries in my letters to the Lord.

Lord,

I always knew that Armando felt like I had nothing to offer. I knew he felt that way before knowing you. Although I thought that it would change eventually, it seems that he only lets me know when he's mad at me. And he is trying to break my spirit. If I'm being honest, it makes me question what I should do. The thing is, there's nothing I can do other than pray. I say that because the minute he apologizes, I'm forced to forget it all. Although I do, I'm questioning what I should be doing. He makes me feel scared & I lose a sense of security, wanting a backup plan in case one day he snaps & wants to end it all. That's one side of me; the other wants to pray endlessly until one day he realizes that I have more to offer than any woman in this world, although I have nothing that this world considers to be success. This is the second time this year that I've feared for my marriage.

I'm not trying to play the victim, Lord, but he knows exactly what to say to hurt me on purpose. I know it's on purpose because it's always the things I've told him about me when I'm trying to be vulnerable. I wish he knew the effect that it has on me. The effects of what a few words can do to me. I haven't been reading your Word lately or as often as I should, which explains why I'm having these thoughts.

He said I had nothing to offer other than my private area, which immediately made me not want to be on this planet. My heart sank. My own husband doesn't see any value in me. It's my fault, though. I shouldn't have said what I said. It was a dumb joke but quickly turned sideways when he tried to burn me back. I shouldn't find any type of validation from him; it should be from you, Lord, but how do I do that? I need you, Jesus. I don't want to think these thoughts. Help me be a better wife.

IV – ARMANDO

Even when guys in the military would invite me to church back in Okinawa, I thought they were dweebs. I didn't get it. The church community seemed so strange and lame. *Why would I want to make myself smaller or submit to some invisible being?* I'd think.

I remembered when a Marine named Pablo came back after leave and was way different. Pablo was in a drunk driving accident, and nearly died. His near-death experience led him to the Lord, and when he came back to Japan, he traded nights partying for nights in his room reading his Bible. He was also demoted. I felt bad for him. He used to be so fun! He was the life of the party. I didn't understand why he'd want to waste his time in Japan in his room, but every time I saw him walking around base with his Bible, the dude was glowing. One day, I'd understand the kind of transformation Pablo had encountered.

But Pearl, the more she read the scripture, the brighter and bigger she became. I could see her change. When I was cruel to her, she wouldn't react. She would go back to her Bible and read and read. I thought it was ridiculous. But I was also intrigued.

I knew Proverbs was "the money book of the Bible," and since I was inhaling books on success and how to build up businesses, I flipped through the book of Proverbs.

One verse that stuck out to me was, "For she's sweet like honey but stings like a viper."

I was supposed to be meeting a woman to start up an affair. She knew I was married. I drove over to this woman's house. She had poured wine, and we were making small talk and suddenly, like a bolt of lightning dropped on my head, I heard that "viper" verse from Proverbs.

In my mind's eye, I saw the image of my wife. How much she loved me and how she was waiting at home for me so unselfishly.

It was almost too heavy to process all at once. I had to get out of there immediately.

"I have to go right now. I can't do this," I said.

I drove back to my wife that night.

When I opened the door, I fell into Pearl's arms. She hugged me and didn't ask any questions.

At that point, the only part of the Bible that I cared about was the parts that taught on how to be prosperous and make money. I treated Scripture like any other self-help text. It was a tool to get me closer to making my dreams a reality.

I never took the time to question *why* I wanted to be successful. I just knew I wanted more out of life. I wanted to be a millionaire by twenty-five. I wanted Ferraris and Lambos, and I was constantly comparing myself to the other content creators online who were killing it with their channels. I had the drive for a bigger life, but I had never answered the "why." Why do I want a million dollars? Why do I want cars and women? I thought it would make me happy. But I had achieved those things in the past and knew intrinsically that none of that mattered. It didn't make me fulfilled or happy.

Thankfully, Scripture is not self-help. It is the living Word of God, and even though I was reading it like a textbook, the Holy Spirit was able to speak to me. Add to that the prayers of Pearl.

I became curious about the Bible. I wanted to see if more than just Proverbs was impactful. So, just like every other thing I had learned in my life of great significance, the first place I went to learn about the Lord was YouTube.

I binge-watched apologetic videos and sermons. I watched Christian versus atheist debates and heard what people from all sorts of walks of faith believed. I wanted to know about different faiths and kept coming back to Christianity.

It didn't happen overnight, and I wasn't transformed in the snap of my fingers. But seeds were planted and began taking root.

As the Lord convicted my heart, I realized I was going to have to make significant changes.

The first thing that needed to change was where I was working. I had created another larger-than-life persona for myself. Even though I was killing it in the apartment business, the job left me vulnerable to pursue relationships with a lot of single women.

I was hoping God's promises were real, but it was still so difficult for me to accept that there was an all-loving Creator out there. I went down every rabbit hole you can possibly go down on the internet to prove or disprove Christianity. And eventually, the love of God clicked in my heart and soul.

It doesn't matter how much research you do. Something in your heart knows the words of Jesus Christ are the real deal.

Pearl and I decided it was time for us to get out of the apartment industry and level up to houses. Selling houses is a completely different landscape. You're dealing with mostly families, couples, and people with more stability than those buying apartments.

Plus, I wanted to remove myself from temptation and keep myself from getting into trouble. While I may not have outright said it, I no longer wanted to be with other women. That was a shift I recognize in hindsight. And the seeds of God's love continued to grow.

I also started learning how God uses ALL things for the good of those who love Him. I started to think of ways I could use these natural gifts God had given me to make a good life for my family. I asked myself, *How can I take the lessons I've learned as a content creator and the lessons I've learned in the military to create a business that survives the test of time?*

I reached out to my Mom and asked her if she could teach me how to sell houses. We went to an open house listing, and I brought my secret weapon: a new camera.

When we met the listing agent, she gave us a confused look.

"Where's your client?" she asked.

"It's just us. I'm here to film the house, and then I'll put it on social media," I told the agent.

"Um, no," the agent was immediately flustered. "This is a waste of my time. How is a video going to sell this house?" she blurted out.

I couldn't convince her to let me film, but eventually, Mom and I found someone who let me film. I started recording model homes.

Later that day, I posted the video online. At the time, realtors weren't fully utilizing social media. Some agents had swanky profiles but rarely put in the effort to make a high-quality video to showcase a listing.

I continued this way for weeks—putting all the things I had learned on You-Tube over the years into place. I posted home tours daily, often getting laughed at or even kicked out of the listings. I was creating something for someone other than myself. I felt like there was a bigger picture.

Then history started to repeat itself. I reached out to a guy online who had a luxury listing—a half-a-million-dollar home—and I asked if he'd be interested in me doing a house tour listing of his home.

This guy gave me a chance. I only had a few hundred followers on social media at the time, but I was posting new content every day.

"Sure thing, man!" he said and gave me a key to his listing.

I filmed his house. It was a gorgeous modern home. I posted the video online. In the middle of the night, my phone started vibrating like crazy. This video got over a million views, and my follower count went from 100 something to 25,000 overnight. Not only that, but my inbox was filled with people asking for homes. I woke up Pearl.

"Look! Look! We are going viral!" I showed her the channel.

The next day we had 50,000 followers, and by the end of the week, we had 100,000 followers. Social media success was happening all over again, just like it had with Navathebeast, but this time I wanted to build something to last for my wife and family, and for my new faith in the Lord.

Another significant change happened during this time. My mother and I began to heal our relationship. I knew I couldn't take back the years of arguments and fights, but I could see her with new eyes and more love. I saw her as someone who was also broken, realizing she had done the best with what she had. Healing my relationship with my mother was integral in repairing my view of women. I began to see women as not disposable.

And Mom helped me learn how to sell houses. She was a baller. She helped me through the process of selling my first home, and we made more money in one paycheck than I had in my entire life.

I was in no way perfect. I wouldn't even say I was a Christian at that time, at least, not in an intentional way; I hadn't yet prayed or professed my faith, but I was letting the truths of the love of God wash over me. And the closer I drew to the Lord, through the scriptures, the more laser-focused I became on loving my wife and building something for the both of us.

CHAPTER 9

Killing the Beast

*For we are his workmanship, created in Christ Jesus for good works,
which God prepared beforehand, that we should walk in them.*

—EPHESIANS 2:10

I – PEARL

We didn't become Christians in one sweeping moment; it was slow and steady. We stumbled in the dark, but as the scriptures say, "Thy Word is a Lamp unto our feet a light to our path."

Many people can recount the exact moment they asked Jesus into their heart, but that's not my story. For me, becoming a Christian felt like getting to know my Father for the first time. The more time I spent in scripture, the more I could hear Him calling me, and encouraging me not to give up on my husband.

Don't get me wrong, there were days I almost gave up. It wasn't easy. I was still struggling with anger and loneliness. But I kept coming back to scripture. And I realized that the only way our marriage was going to survive was if I served my Lord first.

And let me tell you, if you ask Jesus for more love, He will give it to you, and it's a kind of love that is infectious.

I shared what I was learning with my husband, but I knew I couldn't convince him of God's love. I knew he needed to have his own encounter with the Holy Spirit. So, I would pray and dream about our lives on the other side.

As a quiet, reserved person, I began to understand my life's purpose was to be a witness to my husband. I could see how natural it was for him to connect with people and realized we could have an incredible opportunity to use our lives to further The Kingdom of Heaven. I didn't have to go to a mission field in another country; my mission field was my home. I made it my job to be a witness to my husband. To fight for him and his soul.

The closer I grew with the Lord, the less I reacted to Armando's anger or internalized his behavior. Our house became calmer. Armando became calmer too.

I never beat him over the head with the Bible.

I did leave it on the nightstand, though.

And one day, he picked it up.

The more he read, the more he grew in amazement of God and His bigger plan. And slowly but surely, Armando started to see things differently.

Baptism was a beautiful experience, but I was still struggling with God's grace. I was convicted of my past sins, but old thought patterns kept creeping up. For so much of my life, I lived with shame. When I'd hear sermons about how we are Christ's bride, holy and sanctified, I really struggled to believe I could ever measure up. I didn't see myself as holy at all. I had felt so much shame after years of abuse that it was hard to picture my body as something pure.

As a couple, we were gradually learning about God's character, that it has nothing to do with us. He is what makes us clean.

But we live in a fallen world, and the enemy definitely knows our weaknesses.

Armando and I were still in our early days of marriage and new Christians when getting ready for sleep one night, I heard Armando close the bathroom door. My heart sank. I knew what was about to go down. He was going to go watch porn. It's hard to talk about as a wife because it's so common, and on the one hand, you think, *well, at least it's not a real person he's sleeping with.* But I knew my husband. He'd spent so many years of his life living online in a fantasy world, and that escapism could become totally intoxicating. It seeped into his real day-to-day life.

As someone who has had to fight to feel secure my whole life, it took me down a peg to think of him fantasizing about another woman. It impacted our sex life too. It's hard to keep porn out of the marriage bedroom. There were times he couldn't even look at me during sex because he wanted me to be someone else. He'd cover my face or ask me to do things I wasn't totally comfortable with. I wanted to make him happy, so I'd try to be open-minded, but the expectations were unrealistic. When the marriage bedroom is inspired by online scenes, it's set up for heartache.

During that time, I learned that God could transform every single part of my marriage—even the bedroom.

As we became closer to the Lord, I became more comfortable talking to Armando about his porn addiction. As I established trust through self-giving love, he knew I wasn't coming to him in judgment.

One night I talked to him about pornography and something really beautiful happened. Instead of the angry and defensive man I had dated, he was a man full of remorse and ready to own his actions. Instead of cutting me off, he repented and let me become even closer to him by asking for my help.

Dear Heavenly Father,

Last night I found out my husband doesn't think about me when we are making love. That broke my heart and left me speechless. A lot of truth came out of last night. I'm glad he told me because we can work on it with you by our side. I pray that our hearts get closer to you, my lord. I pray the enemy lets him go. I know the enemy wants to take our marriage down. We won't let that happen. Help us, father. I pray our marriage is stronger. In Jesus's name, amen.

From that night, he let me in. I'd get a text or a call from my husband asking me to pray for him because he was in the middle of a battle. Our battles are different. Mine were internal; the way I viewed myself, I tended to self-destruct inward, thinking I was a piece of garbage. For Armando, it was an outward destruction where he would run back to the garbage.

But we learned that the more honest he was, the more we could work on healing that part of our marriage. It took time, to be honest. It's a life commitment. This vulnerable sharing is something we continue to do and something we continue to invite God into.

I had to rely on Jesus to know how to navigate that part of our marriage. I wrote letters asking the Lord to heal us. Forgiving wasn't as difficult as forgetting. That's the way the enemy tried to get me. I wrestled with ruminating on all of the lies. Like, *Your husband doesn't really love you, you're not good enough.*

Dear Jesus,

Thank you for getting us here safely. Lord, I've been battling. It's been four days since Armando confessed all the things he did in our early marriage before giving our lives to you. It was easy to forgive him, but it is hard to forget. Just when I thought I had conquered all the insecurities, they all came back as if an almost healed wound reopened. Now, I find myself questioning things like, Does he find me attractive, and being extra careful with what I say because the minute he makes a face, I immediately think he dislikes me. Lord, I need you. I need your healing love. I know these thoughts aren't yours. It's part of the sanctification that we went through, but I can't lie; I do hurt now, and the thoughts flood.

During this time, Armando and I were still living in San Antonio, and he was posting house tour videos online. And while we were going through such a change in our home, I would have never imagined the kind of change that was in store for both of us just one month later.

II – ARMANDO

God loves me.

What?

How can that be true?

Yeah right.

A perfect God would send his son to die for me?

My own family couldn't even deal with me as a kid. How am I supposed to believe that this perfect being wants anything to do with me?

Oh, and he wants me to be blameless? Great. Has He seen my track record? How many mistakes have I made?

Those are just some of the words I'd mull over when I'd read the Bible. I wanted to be loved, but it was hard for me to believe that God would give away his love for free. What's the catch? When will the rug get pulled out from under me? I just didn't trust it.

I didn't grow up in the church, so the beauty of the free gift of salvation was a mystery to me. It seemed impossible. I felt like a lost stray dog—too dirty to come inside. And yet, there is this master of a gorgeous house who's opened the front door and left a big juicy steak on the welcome mat. And I devour it. And it's the best thing I've ever eaten.

"That is just a taste of what I have in store for you," says the master, "Come inside, I'll make you clean."

I'm a filthy dog. I can't come inside, I thought. And I could often hear the howling of the other wild dogs calling me back to the streets, encouraging me to return to the familiar taste of garbage.

There were times I rejected the master's invitation inside and went back to the dumpster looking for garbage. But I began to learn that the invitation was not a one-time offer. It is a gift to us.

When Jesus invited me inside, I was hesitant. But, you know, scripture isn't another "how to" book. It's alive. It is the Word of God. I didn't realize when I was picking up the book that I was opening myself up for a Road to Damascus experience. It's only by the supernatural work of God that this is possible because, man, if it were up to me, I'd probably still be out there trying to eat garbage.

Those scriptures that were planted in my heart began to grow.

I saw Jesus's love for me first through my own wife. When I was cruel, and she stayed by my side, I interpreted her faithfulness as ignorance. But eventually I realized she was operating on a whole different level.

It broke my heart wide open. To feel her love was also to feel Christ's love for me.

One day I woke up and stopped questioning if her love was real. I stopped trying to test her and put her through hell. I realized her love was coming from somewhere higher and more powerful than anything I could really understand. And I craved that love.

I devoured the scriptures. I mean hours and hours of reading. I couldn't get enough. Slowly, I began to trust in God's promises. Everything started to sink in and fall into place.

It was like I had been making myself sick for years, eating a smoothie with old rotten fruit. Once Jesus's love took hold of me, I wanted to blend up something new and delicious made with fresh fruit—the blend of his Word, Lordship/friendship, and community.

The other part of my life that needed to be transformed was my marriage. I had seen commitment as a burden. And I had viewed Pearl with resentment, an entity that was holding me back from something greater.

How wrong was I! She was my precious Pearl. My gift from God, praying for me in the background the entire time. I wanted to know how to be a better husband and build something to last with her.

Our marriage started to grow, and I started opening up. We had many hurdles; I asked for her forgiveness for things I had done early in our relationship and marriage. For wanting to be with other women, all of it.

The spirit is willing, but the flesh is weak.

As I steadily gave more and more of my heart to Christ, I started to see my past behavior differently. I grieved over my sins.

Where I had felt most "god-like" was in the bedroom. Before I became a Christian, I felt the most in control and the most ecstasy when I was with a woman. I loved the thrill of the chase. Pursuing women felt like playing chess —there was strategy and a game.

But as I started seeking the Lord, I realized I needed to let those addictions die.

After Pearl and I got married, I was prepared to not sleep with other women—that was an obvious no-no. But early on in my dating and marriage, I didn't see a problem with porn and chatting with other women online.

I had lived so much of my life escaping into my own online world, and porn was another one of those worlds. It wasn't "real" sex. It wasn't hurting anyone. But like any addiction, I found I needed to continue coming back to it over and over. And it was never enough.

It wasn't until I saw the way my fantasies were impacting my wife that I realized I needed to kill that beast.

I began confessing everything to Pearl. I didn't want to hurt her. I wanted her to understand and help me. Those demons. That lust. The need to be in control and be my own god. I had struggled with those addictions since I was a kid. It was going to take much more than my own willpower to let go.

I started throwing myself into accomplishments outside of sex. I wanted to be a better husband, to be good at my job, to put energy into things that were greater than myself.

I also took inventory of where I was most easily tempted and systematically began cutting things out of my life that could cause me to stumble. I had to create boundaries and literally move out of temptations to fight for my faith and my marriage.

I learned early on that every single day there would be an opportunity to stumble. I began to understand the "fear of the Lord is the beginning of wisdom" and saw my path more clearly. There's a spirit way and a flesh way forward. So, when I'd want to run back to the garbage dump, I'd stop in my tracks and pray. I began to realize that lust, sex, and power are things we encounter daily in this world. I learned to arm myself with the full armor of God and be ready to do battle. Otherwise I'd get taken out.

I had already blocked many porn websites, stopped watching R-rated movies and TV shows that weren't edifying. I'd ignored and blocked women in my inbox, but it didn't matter how much I tried to limit myself in my own strength. I could see the most random post on Instagram and get sucked back into wanting to hook up.

Things didn't significantly change, and my addictions didn't start to loosen until I truly started viewing myself as a soldier in the army of God. Once that clicked in for me—that we don't wrestle against flesh and blood but against principalities—things really shifted. All the military training and discipline I had put towards being part of an earthly army I applied to the Lord's heavenly army.

And then all the good things I learned in the military came back to me. The military changed my perception of competition. In the Marine Corps, the structure, the organization, and the task-oriented schedule helped me foster a sense of competition that I'd not had before.

When I think about how I essentially lived unkempt in that utility closet as a kid, I shudder. Post-military life, I can't even imagine going a few days without shaving let alone not taking a shower. That life changed me for the better. And thankfully, God picked up where the lessons from the military ended.

As a Christian, I began serving as part of a team for a bigger purpose. It felt like my military training. I was able to receive a sense of meaning that I was craving since I took my uniform off. I had a clear image of who I was serving and a clear picture of our mission. So, when I started to serve the Lord, I did it with my entire heart. I wanted to give it my all like I had done during my time in the military. With my military mentality, everything I did was geared towards bringing honor and glory to Him. And if, as scripture says, the Word of God is a sword, then if I was to win the battle, I was going to sharpen mine.

Pearl and I began memorizing scriptures.

I opened my phone to the Navathebeast channel. I'd been posting here and there on the YouTube channel since I left the military. After I gave my life to the Lord, I felt like all the Navathebeast videos and posts didn't represent me anymore. The more I dug into scripture, the more those layers of my old persona were shedding like snakeskin.

It got to a point where I didn't want those videos out in the ether. What if someone went to the channel and started to look at me as all that? Plus, the women and the toxic behavior that came from the channel. I was ready for it to be over.

But it felt like killing a part of me, like putting an animal down.

It's time to end this, I thought, as my finger hovered over my computer mouse.

My heart began to pound like a war drum while I scrolled through countless videos I'd posted online over the last decade of my life.

My YouTube channel, *Navathebeast,* was the first official military influencer account and garnered millions of views and subscribers. That kind of influence translated into fame on camera and a pile of cash and women off camera. At one time, I enjoyed the spoils of my online empire. But like most empires, it wouldn't last. There was no foundation laid down for the hollow house I had built.

I muted the volume on my computer. I felt disgusted listening to the youthful voice behind the high-energy YouTube persona I had created.

The man on camera was the spitting image of Armando Nava. We had the same features, hair, and laugh. But we were not the same person. Not anymore.

I could see myself aging as I scrolled down the channel. There were good memories too, and so many good opportunities to connect with people around the world. But I had built this empire on a foundation of sand.

I breathed in and closed my eyes.

"You can do this," Pearl said gently, rubbing my shoulder. "We can do this. God will provide."

The yellow glow of the computer bounced off her face, and I saw my videos in the reflection of her glasses. An influencer shutting down their own social media account is like a baker setting fire to their own bakery. My social media accounts were more than my business, they were my entire identity.

Suddenly, I was reminded of the verse in 2 Corinthians:

"Therefore, if anyone is in Christ, he is a new creation. The old has passed away; behold, the new has come." 2 Corinthians 5:17

I took one final glance at the collection of usernames and comments underneath some of my favorite videos.

Ok. Let's go!

Click, click, click.

"This will permanently delete your YouTube data," the pop-up screen said.

A blue box with the words "Delete my Content" was one click away.

DELETE.

We shut it down. I terminated my account.

When I deleted the channel, it felt like I could fully commit to my wife and my Lord. I didn't have to live in both worlds. I felt a weight lift, a huge sense of relief, like all the chains were broken and I could finally move forward!

Behold the new creation. The old has passed away, and the new has come!

CHAPTER 10

Pharisee Mindset

".... so be as wise as serpents and yet as harmless as doves.
But be on your guard against men."
—MATTHEW 10:16

I – ARMANDO

Ok, so here's where things get a little crazy.

We accidentally joined a cult.

Well, kinda.

Let me backtrack a little.

We were new Christians smack-dab in the middle of the COVID-19 pandemic. Churches had shuttered their doors, and communities were meeting for online worship services. Pearl and I didn't start our journey with a group of believers. We were often in our own prayer closet, in our own home, reading scripture and asking the Holy Spirit to guide us.

We were still searching for Godly leaders to help us interpret the Bible and support us during our new walk, but as the world went inside during the pandemic, we had to rely on our old tool for community: YouTube.

I used YouTube to learn how to build my business and how to pick up girls. So why not use it to understand Christianity?

There is good stuff online as well. Learning about our faith through the internet was an incredible gift. We heard sermons from seasoned Pastors and Reverends from every corner of the world and connected with other Christians across denominations. But the difficult thing about exploring faith online as a new Christian is that we also got exposed to a lot of unsound doctrine.

When I became a Christian, I wanted to be part of God's army. I don't do things halfway, so I wanted to follow the rules and be me in this community of Christians.

The COVID-19 virus was killing people, and the world felt so unsafe. It truly did feel like the end of times. And as we soaked in the Word, we also were paying attention to the Promise that Jesus would return. And when we read the Book of Revelation and looked out our window in the time of the pandemic, we thought, *This must be the apocalypse.* Wow! Lord Jesus must be coming back this year!

I found myself binge-watching videos on The End Times when Jesus would come back to Earth as He promised.

I'd share the videos with Pearl, and we'd spend hours talking about how current events lined up with what we were reading in the Bible. And we had plenty of hours.

Soon, we became freaked out by everything. We believed one wrong move could send us to Hell, and we wanted to cut out everything that could keep us from entering Heaven.

The messages Pearl and I were drawn to were severe. We were in a fear loop. God is coming back, and we have to be ready. But what we didn't understand about Jesus was that it's not by our hands but by his spirit we are saved. We thought we could control our salvation by being as pure and good as possible.

We stopped watching TV and listening to secular music. (Even now, we don't listen to secular music and are careful about the kind of shows we consume.)

We quit shopping for nice clothes and decided we should only wear cheap clothes from Walmart. The logic behind that was if Jesus is coming back, we don't need to invest in anything of this world, especially luxury items. Plus, we wanted our outward appearance to match the changes that were going on inside.

We were making decisions out of fear. I'd wake up in the middle of the night to a cold sweat, horrified that Jesus was going to return and I wasn't going to be prepared.

"I'm not good enough to go to Heaven," I would say to Pearl. "Babe, I'm not saved; how am I gonna get to Heaven?" Then we'd cry together and recount our sins. And we'd think there's no way for a perfect God to let us in.

When I looked in the mirror, I knew I needed to be saved by something bigger than myself. But I didn't understand the deep and endless well of love and forgiveness Jesus had for me. I thought I was going to have to do more for him to love me.

We didn't understand that "perfect love drives out all fear." At that point in our lives, our faith was still rooted in a lot of fear and shame. We feared hell, sin, and the end of times. We wanted to earn our salvation by proving to the Lord how sincere we were. Looking back, that was a recipe for disaster. Our hearts were in the right place, as we were open, but we had not yet learned to rest in the Lord's love.

"Leave your home and follow me," Scripture says. So, we started selling everything we owned.

First, we sold my Mercedes for a beat-up old truck. Then I quit shaving and caring about how I looked. We tried to live as simply as possible.

We also stopped going to our family's *carne asadas* and get-togethers. We didn't want to be around people who were drinking. We started to take on a "holier than thou" attitude. We didn't know how to accept God's grace for ourselves, and we definitely didn't know how to offer grace to our families. They already thought we were a little nuts and becoming religious only added to that. Especially when we started pushing the Gospel down our family's throats. We had seen such an incredible transformation in our marriage and career that we wanted to share the message with our families, but we had no chill—no grace.

We even stopped going to holiday functions, like Thanksgiving. We tried to weasel our way out of Christmas, but our family pushed us to participate. So, what did we buy our relatives for Christmas presents? *Bibles.* Yeah, we weren't subtle with our faith.

We were green. So green. We wanted to do everything we could to serve the Lord with our entire lives and were looking for role models online. It was in this frame of mind that we first encountered Pastor Jacob's YouTube Channel.

Our faith was so open, and we soaked his hellfire and brimstone messages in.

Pastor Jacob's videos were suggested to us via the YouTube algorithm. He would mostly read from the Book of Revelation and tell his viewers to prepare for the End Times. His messages caught us at a time when we were consumed with earning our salvation. Jacob put a strong emphasis on modesty and temperance. We were so preoccupied with losing our faith and being "left behind" in the Rapture, that we clung to his every word.

Turns out, Jacob was only three hours away from us in San Antonio. He was preparing for the End Times on his ranch. So, I reached out to Jacob and asked how we could prepare for Jesus's return.

He invited us to his church on his ranch and said that he could reserve a spot for us at his RV park.

With the pandemic happening all around us, and our fear on full blast, Pearl and I literally bought an RV and headed to the desert the same day. Pearl watched videos online to learn how to maintain the RV. We had no idea what we were getting into, but we felt an urgency to prove that we were serious about Jesus's return.

We also bought a ton of survival packages and cans of food from preppers online. I think we still have cans of beans in our basement.

Jacob's theory was that the world was only going to get darker and crazier before the Lord's return. He believed the COVID-19 vaccine was the *Mark of the Beast* and told us that anyone who was vaccinated would be separated from God forever. Looking back, it sounds crazy, but at that time, there was so much uncertainty. Add to that, we were so ready to believe and be good Christians. So, we believed him.

We left everything and moved to the desert in an RV to ride out the end of the world with Pastor Jacob.

II – PEARL

"Welcome," said Pastor Jacob as we pulled up the long dusty road with our new RV.

I wasn't sure if selling everything we had and moving to the desert was the wisest decision we could make, but I was open because of the huge changes I had seen in my husband. He wanted to make moves for the Lord and for the Kingdom of Heaven and not for his personal gains. He was transforming into the man I had been praying for so fervently this whole time. So, when he suggested moving to the desert, I thought, *Ok, this must be some kind of answer to my prayer*. I was open to it because of the changes I had seen.

Pastor Jacob was a towering man with a long white beard. At first, he reminded me of Santa Claus. He maintained his ranch with his wife, Sue, who was demure and warm.

The ranch was in the middle of nowhere, and in the center of the land was a little white church.

After Jacob and Sue showed us to our parking spot, they invited us to their church.

When we walked in, I could smell the old wood and dusty air. It could hold about fifty people, like a church from the olden times. It was comforting. I found it peaceful.

But then there was the TV screen down by the altar. On the TV screen, there was the number "666" talking about the End of the World. It was jarring to see those kinds of images, but we filed it away and dove into our new life.

There was another couple on the ranch. Sarah and Joshua. They, like us, had found Pastor Jacob online and had come to live a simple life out on the ranch until Jesus returned.

He preached an intense sermon that brought me to tears and filled me with fear.

Afterwards, we went back to our RV and looked around our new home. We had a bed, a small bathroom, a loveseat, a simple kitchen, a few pots and pans, our survival food, and miles and miles of Texas skyline. We were seriously off the grid.

The next day, we woke up at 4:00 a.m. Early rising wasn't hard on the ranch when the huge orange sun is as big as the entire sky. Plus, we didn't have a lot to do and had gone to bed early. We drove to a gym about thirty minutes away.

Armando was still posting house tour videos online. So, a few times a week we'd drive back to San Antonio, take a bunch of videos of listings, post them while we had solid internet, and then drive back to our RV on the ranch.

At first, we'd go back to our apartment through the weekdays, but eventually, we started spending more time on the ranch. We were chronically exhausted during that period of life, from the long commute and from fasting.

We would fast for up to four to seven days. And then we would binge eat. Rinse, repeat.

We wanted to be in the Spirit and be totally dead to our physical bodies. Every day we'd wake up and Armando would say, "Today is the day the Lord is coming, I can feel it."

Several times a week, we'd have church with Jacob and the others on the ranch. After a few months, I felt like we had heard everything four times. Jacob's sermons sounded like prerecorded scripts and had cold undertones. In the time that we were there, I don't remember a time he spoke about Jesus's love or the Father's provision, or the comfort of the Holy Spirit. His message was always concerned with the End Times.

We felt like the world was going to end. We were literally working to pass time.

He never confronted us, but we always felt like we were coming up short. Like we needed to do more and more to earn our salvation.

Appeasing Jacob was not easy, but we felt it was a small sacrifice compared to the significant gains we were making in our marriage.

For the first time in our lives, Armando and I were completely away from distractions and left to truly deal with our demons. It was just the two of us commuting to and from the desert, sunup to sundown.

When we'd go to San Antonio, we'd spend most of our time reading the Bible, praying, and truly getting to know each other.

During that time, Armando confessed to me that he had been carrying on with another woman during the first few weeks of our marriage. We dove into his fears about commitments, and his attitudes about women. I listened with an open heart and felt compelled to forgive and love him. It was the break-through I had been praying for.

Armando was also able to hold me closer and hear my story in a new way too. The abuse and the grief I had experienced as a young child was something I could share with him. His heart broke for me, and he grieved for the pain I had experienced as a child with Jose.

In fact, we both had so much more capacity for each other's pain. Because of our pasts, we had built up protective walls and shut off our empathetic hearts. It was like we had been living on autopilot and in survival mode for years. I had turned inward into sadness, and he had turned outward into anger. But that all changed in the desert when we turned our hearts towards the Lord. In the middle of the desert, we started over. Praise God.

When we began to look at the arch of our lives, we were filled with so much thankfulness. So many times, we had been inches from death and destruction. We could see God's hand on our lives.

III – ARMANDO

Our family struggled with our decision to go to the desert. Rightly so, they were worried. They believed we had joined a cult and, in some ways, we had. We believed our family was going to hell, and they believed we were wasting our lives with a Doomsday Cult.

Jacob encouraged us to limit time with people who are nonbelievers or who received the vaccine.

But it can be very confusing because there is a scripture where Jesus seems to say, *Leave your family and follow me.* But for new Christians, it's incredibly confusing.

When Pearl told Jacob that her mother had been vaccinated so she could go visit Cuba, he said she wouldn't be able to get into Heaven, and there was nothing we could do for her. That didn't sit right with us.

My Mom was concerned for us, too. We invited her to the ranch, and she made the three-hour-long drive out to the middle of nowhere to have church with us.

Mom has never been religious, but she has always been open-minded. She sat with us through Pastor Jacob's sermon.

After the sermon, we walked out of the church with Mom and Jacob. Mom was wearing a tight dress that was showing a lot of cleavage, and as we said our goodbyes, Jacob said firmly, "The next time you come to my church, you shouldn't wear something so revealing."

He then went on to explain how godly women should clothe themselves in modesty.

I wish I could say I stuck up for my Mom, but at the time, we also believed that the way we dressed could earn us a ticket to Hell or to Heaven. And I was genuinely concerned that my Mom was going to hell, so I didn't question Jacob's extreme words.

My mom is such a class-act. She looked down at her dress, and said, "You're right, Pastor. I shouldn't be wearing this," and she smiled, and we hugged her goodbye.

Mom wanted to try to understand what we were doing with our time out on the ranch. I think she was also worried we were going to wind up in a Jonestown or Waco situation. She came to visit often.

After one church service, she told us what she really thought.

"I think this is weird. And this is also how people die," she said bluntly.

At the time, it was hard for Pearl and me to understand. How can a guy who cares about our souls be dangerous?

Mom was impressed by the change she had seen in my demeanor, but she was concerned with our extremism, and ultimately, she missed us.

After Mom left, Jacob told us we should continue to limit time with loved ones who had been vaccinated. He felt like vaccinated people had received the mark of the beast and were beyond God's redemption.

I couldn't accept Hell for everyone I loved. So, Pearl and I started a Bible study for people back in San Antonio. It was our hope that we could save as many souls as possible. If Jesus was coming back, we had to tell everyone immediately. We were afraid for our souls and for the people whom we loved. We were literally like, "Y'all pack your bags, you need to move out to the desert with us and ride out this apocalypse."

First, our cousins came to our Bible studies, and then some of the people we worked with joined. We mimicked the fire and brimstone messages we had learned from Jacob.

We had seen God move in our lives, and we wanted to share the good news with as many people as possible. But we had no grace at this point. We didn't understand how to let the word take root naturally in the lives of our families. We'd even kick people out of our Bible study who weren't totally Christian. We had a member who always wanted to talk about Buddha, and I wanted this group to be focused on becoming closer to God. So, I literally kicked him out.

A few weeks after we started our bible study, Pearl and I started to have a strange feeling about life on the ranch. But we didn't want to admit it to each other or discourage one another. So, we kept it to ourselves.

At that point we had lived on the ranch for several months and were making the six-hour round trip several times a week between our Bible study and my house tours.

Thank God for giving us His living word. The more we read our Bibles, the more Pearl and I realized how extreme Pastor Jacob's messages were compared to the message of Jesus. And it didn't sit right with me. The more we read scripture, the more we saw a compassionate and forgiving God. Our growing understanding of Jesus didn't match the God that Jacob had us believe was in control.

He said everyone was going to Hell. Children, vaccinated people, everyone but us.

And then, one evening at the church, we walked in to find Jacob upset.

"Where's Sarah and Joshua?" Pearl asked.

"They couldn't handle the truth. They've gone back to the world," he replied.

Sarah and Joshua had left the ranch. They never announced their departure; they just left. And their exit felt significant to us. Especially since we knew them to be kind-hearted and sincere Christians who were trying to live their lives for the Lord. Why would Jacob believe that these people were going to Hell? It didn't add up.

Why would he be speaking so ill of people, who, like us, were trying to decipher God's will for their lives? They had removed themselves from the world, sought God, lived humbly, and they were still going to Hell? Something was off.

IV – PEARL

We were having doubts about Jacob's messages and if we were making the right decision living on the ranch. Then we got a call from Juan Ramos and knew we needed to leave immediately.

Juan was an author and content creator who shared his testimony online. Juan was an ex-Satanist, and we loved hearing his sermons. We had watched his videos and soaked up his theology before moving to the ranch.

But his call wasn't about the apocalypse; it was about buying a house.

Juan was considering moving to Dallas and had seen Armando's real estate channel. He was hoping Armando could help him find a home in Dallas.

I'll never forget when Armando hung up the phone with Juan. He looked at me and said, "Babe, why is Juan buying a house if it's going to be the end of the world?"

I paused and said something that had been gnawing at my heart.

"What if it's *not* the end of the world?"

That's when it dawned on us: If a guy who was so mature in the faith, a man steeped in scripture, was investing in a property on "this Earth," then what were we missing? Why wasn't this guy riding out the apocalypse with us on the ranch?

That's when we took a hard look at Jacob's theology. Many of his messages didn't add up, and we felt pressure to tithe to the church.

We had worked ourselves up with so much fear that we were convinced the Lord was going to come in the middle of the night. We'd literally leave messages on our family's phones and make videos of ourselves saying goodbye, just in case we got raptured in the middle of the night. He fed into our fears and stoked our paranoia. And, after Sarah and Joshua left, we began to feel we also needed to leave before something dangerous could happen.

Juan's call was the tipping point; it reframed our perspective.

We didn't know anything about the Dallas real estate market, but Armando was determined to learn so he could help Juan find a home. Dallas is much bigger than San Antonio and sounded like another adventure.

The only thing standing in our way was Jacob.

We called Armando's mom and told her we needed to leave ASAP. She didn't even ask questions; she was ready to dive in and help us leave the desert.

We packed up everything in black trash bags and drove down the dirt road to the gate, where Jacob was waiting.

"So, duty calls," Armando said. "We are going to Dallas."

We could tell Jacob was not pleased, and we could sense his disappointment.

There was a brief conversation, and eventually Jacob opened the gate, and we drove off the ranch and back to our senses.

I've always bristled at calling the church on the ranch a cult, because God met us there and, in many ways, we grew in our relationship with God and each other. Add to that there are things Jacob preached that are Biblically sound. But his messages were not rooted in Christ's love, and for people like Armando and I, who were vulnerable and new Christians, it could have been a dangerous situation. We were fasting, weak in the body, and persuadable. It's not hard to see how these groups could go off the rails. We were both desperate for father figures and clinging to rules we could impose on ourselves to make up for our past sins. So yeah, I guess it was a cult.

V – (PEARL AND ARMANDO)

Our time in the desert was a detour. We were lucky to have survived. Again, the Lord brought us out of another difficult situation.

But we truly believed God uses all things for the Good of those who love him, even bizarre detours can be used for his Glory. In the desert we learned that "Perfect love casts out all fear." The more we grew in God's love, the more we clung to Jesus, the more we let go of fear and control, and the more we were able to see a way to live fully on this Earth as it is in heaven.

Finally, for the first time in our lives, we decided to quit being preoccupied with death. Death, which had chased us both and called to us since we were children. Instead, we moved to Dallas to learn how to live a spirit-filled life—the more abundant life Jesus talked about and promised us. Yes, we are waiting for Jesus to return. And until this, we are learning to live on Earth as it is in heaven. And thankfully, we don't have to live that way in isolation.

In fall 2023, we were busy in our careers and working on this very book you are reading, when we received a text from Sue. We had kept in contact with her over the years. She informed us that her husband, Pastor Jacob, had died. Our hearts broke for her, and we decided to visit her.

It was a bit surreal to roll up on the ranch again—so much had changed in our lives since we were last here. (You'll read about those changes in the upcoming chapters.)

Sue told us Pastor Jacob had become ill early in 2023 and had spent time reflecting on many things—including his time with us. She said he spoke of us often. And that brought tears to Pearl's eyes.

We don't hold a grudge against Pastor Jacob. Although his hardline version of Christianity didn't inspire us to stay with him on the ranch, we learned a great deal about the Lord out in the desert. And to be honest, we could have ended up just like him. We were zealous and wanted to earn our salvation. We've grown since then and experienced the Lord's forgiveness, healing, comfort, and joy.

We praise God for bringing us out of the desert and into abundant life!

In Dallas we hoped to finally start *living* for God. Really living. Not just surviving. Not just waiting, but actually walking into a life full of joy.

CHAPTER 11

New Mission Field

But seek first the kingdom of God and his righteousness,
and all these things will be added to you.

—MATTHEW 6:33

I – ARMANDO

The desert was like our training ground. God was preparing us before we ended up moving to Dallas. It was perfect timing. We were still very zealous, but we began to internalize Jesus's message of forgiveness and shake off the doubts we had about the Lord's love for us. We also started paying attention to some of the biblical heroes. Think about the lives of Abraham and David. They were called by God but weren't perfect people either. They were used by the Lord, but they still failed. And God actually *spoke* to them.

Driving from the desert into Dallas felt like waking up from sleep. Everything was brand new.

We settled in a little one-bedroom apartment. Life was still simple. Then we started learning about the Dallas real estate market from scratch. I continued filming home tours and posting them online. My real estate social media account was attracting new clients from all over the world. Pearl and I were doing so much better as a couple, too. I wanted to spend more time with her. I wanted to cherish her.

Even though our business was growing online, we decided this time we were going to have boundaries with our relationship to social media. We'd post our videos, interact with clients, and then put our phones away. It sounds so simple, but not being glued to the constant feedback loop of the internet was tremendously helpful for our marriage and our walks with the Lord.

It felt like I could *hear* for the first time because there wasn't so much noise. I'd trade time on my phone for time in the Bible and in prayer. And we made sure to rest on Sundays (which is usually a big workday for most realtors). As a natural workaholic, that was a completely different approach for me. I naturally want to grind like a machine, but I'd already done that and lost everything. I could see it wasn't sustainable to treat your body and especially your soul like a robot. So, as we built this business in Dallas from the ground up, we poured a foundation to last.

One night, while praying, I asked God, "Lord, why did you give me a desire to work in this industry? I want to do more for you. Help me make this about YOU and not about me."

God is good.

The next day I had a conversation with Pearl about how to build the business for God's Kingdom.

"What if we just put it all out there?" said Pearl.

It sounds simple. Coming out as a Christian real estate agent may not sound like it's that big a deal, but in this industry, you don't talk about religion or politics. I learned from my parents that successful realtors should stay neutral in their beliefs. But as we were steadily making sales, I felt like something was missing. I read about Jesus calling his disciples to leave everything and follow him. He made them "fishers of men." And the disciples went on to live for the Kingdom of Heaven. I wondered: How can Pearl and I glorify Christ in our daily lives? How can we use our business to glorify God?

We felt like our business was a gift from the Lord. It didn't feel like it even belonged to us; it belonged to Christ.

"You're right," I said to Pearl. "Let's just put it out there."

When we chatted with our family and friends about "going public" with our faith, they were concerned.

People will think you're a freak.

This is going to kill your business.

You're going to lose clients.

You can still be Christian realtors and not talk about Jesus.

We were told we'd lose wealthy clients because there's a perception that rich people are less religious. Plus, you could isolate future clients.

It didn't matter to us. We wanted to share this good news with people.

I saw every single client as an opportunity to minister and share the love of the Lord. There's no secret that I am married to Pearl. There's no secret that I am a family man, so why should my Christian walk be a secret? Why would I keep this gift a secret?

Plus, I had deleted my Navathebeast account, and I wasn't beholden to any sort of fake influencer persona. For the first time in my online career, I could speak the way I naturally spoke and connect with people in a new way. I didn't have to be a hype-man or act like I was a dude on speed!

The way I hosted my real estate tours was calm and authentic. With the peace of Christ, I could show my audience a version of me that pointed towards the Lord.

It started small and then grew. And grew.

We'd put a scripture at the bottom of every post. Then, we wrote out our testimony and put it on our website. Eventually, we started recording messages about our faith and incorporating the Gospel in every post.

"Be sure to stay tuned towards the end of the video because we have some good news to share with you. By far, the greatest news you'll ever hear in your life. So, stay tuned," I'd say. And then we would share the Gospel.

"Listen, my friends," I'd say in the videos. "These houses are awesome, but they're temporary. Your body's temporary. This life is temporary, because there's an eternal home that is far greater than any earthly home."

When I heard the word "Shalom" in a sermon, it really resonated in my soul. The Hebrew word is a peaceful greeting. I started saying "shalom" in our videos to welcome every viewer in peace. I wanted to point them to a bigger and better life. Not just the homes we could provide, but the life Jesus could offer them if they had faith in him.

And that's how our Christian real estate business started.

There were definitely haters, and we certainly lost clients initially. Some developers actually backed out after they found out we were Christian. They didn't want to mess with us. We were blacklisted with some people. But we kept it up. During those first few weeks of posting our Christian walks our inbox was flooded with both positive and negative comments. We received a lot of encouragement from other believers to keep up the good work. But sadly, some of the most critical comments we received were also from believers who thought we were using the Lord for our gain.

There was a lot of snarkiness, nastiness, and downright ugliness in our inbox. But it wasn't my first rodeo fielding the cesspool of social media, and this time I was not building up an empire in my own image. Certainly, it upset me when people doubted our sincerity. There were, and still are, times I just want to comment on every single post and say something in our defense. But we are not doing this to please anyone here on earth.

The scripture says, *They will know you're Christian by your fruit.* So let people see how we live, let people see our fruit—that's enough. We can't be concerned with what they are commenting on. We are only concerned with God's view and plan for us.

Plus, we want to see change and revival. We believe ministry is what you do every day. So much of our life is spent in the workplace—so why wouldn't we use that time to share the Gospel where we are, with the people we encounter everyday? We are called to be Salt and Light. And we are asking the Lord to bring the Kingdom down to earth.

"Thy Kingdom come, thy will be done, on earth as it is in heaven."

That's Kingdom language! And we aren't waiting to die to be part of the Kingdom, the Kingdom is here now.

And we hope to be in positions of leadership like the heroes who led nations.

As we studied the scripture and read about these leaders, we noticed how often they failed epically! But heroes like Abraham, Moses, and Joseph clung to the Lord and accomplished huge things for the Kingdom. They didn't have set backs, they had set UPS for what God was preparing them to accomplish.

This is why we wanted to start sharing our story. Because we know what it's like to fail epically, but we also know what it's like to be saved from our sin. And it's Good News we believe everyone needs to hear. We want to shout it from the rooftops, "Jesus is alive. You don't have to feel the sting of death anymore. Praise God!"

II – PEARL

It's a calling. God has called us to do exactly what we are doing.

When we started talking about posting our faith online, it was an obvious choice. Not only did we want to share the love of the Lord with people, but we wanted to be able to help them during what can be an incredibly stressful process. Buying a home is one of the biggest things a family will ever do. It's a major milestone and can be a vulnerable experience.

As people who own our business, we see money as a tool—but we know it is fleeting. We have seen the love of money destroy and know firsthand it does not bring happiness. So, when we started to focus our business on clients over commissions, everything changed. God has always provided our paycheck.

And we learned early on that when we stop obsessing over the commission or over the numbers, then we actually see a huge return.

Armando was sharing the love of Christ with every single client who set up a meeting with him. And he still does.

It's been so life-giving for me to watch my husband use his skills and also draw on his faith to comfort people and offer this sound advice during these vulnerable moments. I have always been a behind-the-scenes person. Since my social battery isn't nearly as long as Armando's, I really enjoy taking care of all of the administration and back-end elements of our business. It's been wonderful to be able to be at home in my own skills, too. I am able to use the talents and skills God gave me to support our business.

There have been many phone calls with tears and even more with prayer. The closing process is extremely emotional. And it's really been an opportunity to share our faith. Waiting on paperwork, deals, contracts—it's deeply personal. It provides a wonderful opportunity to encourage people. If a deal doesn't go through, *don't lose hope. God has a bigger plan for you.* I've seen my husband talk people down from the brink of a panic attack.

It's been so neat to develop strong friendships and be part of a meaningful community together through this business. Some of our clients work with us once, and others have become lifelong friends.

Regardless of whether we become friends or not, we always pray for the home our clients are going to move into because we know that the home is the central foundation to the family. We want to pray for generations of family members who will be growing up in the homes we sell.

I have to give thanks to my Lord who has answered so many of my prayers!

Beyond growing our business, the Lord has blessed my marriage. Armando and I share the same vision for our future and have enjoyed building something together. It's such a gift to get to work with your spouse. Sure, we have off days and long days. But it's a blessing to be totally aligned in the spirit. Praise God!

III – ARMANDO

I still remember one of the texts I received after speaking about the Lord with a client. I wasn't nervous about sharing my faith, but it was still new terrain for me.

"I would love to work with you. I love the fact that you incorporate God," he said. "I'm so happy that I met somebody that actually cares."

I texted back, "All glory to Christ."

When you declare yourself a Christian business, every conversation is going to be remembered a little bit differently. If you were to cuss someone out, it's game over. That may be obvious. But what may be less obvious is, if you are inconsiderate or selfish, that's going to come across too.

God is a master creator. Imagine a house here that is like a mansion. No matter how gorgeous the mansion is, a home in Heaven is a million times more stunning. That is the truth that guides how we approach creating our Christian business. If we are going to label our business with this super important word "Christian," then the bar should be set higher than everybody else. Not only in the product but in the service we deliver. Because now we have an explicit responsibility to show people the love of Christ. And we want to be the best representatives of Jesus that we can be.

Every day starts with Pearl and me in the Word. There have been times when a client is driving me nuts, but I need to die to myself and serve them. Wash their feet and love them.

Don't get me wrong, we are human, and we fail all the time. And when we do, we ask God to forgive us. We know that we will be under a microscope, and our actions will be scrutinized because of our open faith. We know there is a bullseye on us, and we want to take the responsibility and calling seriously.

I never worry about spending too much time with an interested client because I see every phone conversation as an opportunity to be a witness to the love of Jesus. I walk new clients through a five-step process. We are building a foundation together! We chat about the process: connecting to a loan officer, the resale factor, good appreciation of homes in their market, etc. I want our clients to be educated buyers because buying a home is a huge financial decision for them. We create an itinerary based on what kind of properties they want to view. Then, when we find their home, we submit their contract and close on the property.

After I give my spiel, I ask the client to pray about the decision to work with us. It's a different approach to sales because I am completely at ease with the client working with someone else. You see, ultimately it is not about me or Pearl. The Lord is working in our lives, and the Lord is working in their lives. It's wonderful when our paths cross and we are able to work together, but since viewing our business as our ministry, we have taken the stress out of retaining new clients—knowing every single step we take is in the Lord's hands.

What's interesting is that clients recognize our hearts. In our fast-paced competitive economy, it's countercultural to go a little slower, to truly get to know clients and be concerned with the person over the commission. The real estate industry can be flashy and obsessed with aesthetics. I mean, of course, we are selling homes, and aesthetics do matter. But when realtors become more concerned with dollar signs and the endless money pit, we are missing out on an opportunity to really connect with our clients and truly help them.

And we've seen, by God's grace, that even unbelievers will want to work with us because of this commitment to love and excellence. We've served clients from all sorts of faiths, too. I recently worked with a man who was Muslim, and we had a great conversation.

Jesus came to love and serve. And as believers leading a Christian business, we are here to do the same. Like Jesus washed his disciples' feet, we are here to serve in the same spirit.

Sometimes it can be a challenge when you get gruff or when clients are rude. Part of being open about our faith is knowing how to humbly speak truth in love. We are still human, and, of course, there are times when we have disagreements with clients.

It was something I had to learn how to navigate. I didn't want to give our clients any reason to doubt the Love of the Lord. So, at first, I would let the clients run all over us. But it's not in the client's best interest if I can't be their advocate. So, I had to learn how to be assertive and strong but also lead with love. It's something I am still learning. Jesus gave us the model. He spoke the truth in love. He didn't let the Sanhedrin run all over him, while at the same time, he gave his life for them—for all of us.

We trust a lot in the Lord. We trust the Lord to put us in contact with the right contacts. When clients drop off, we don't freak out.

And there have been clients we decided not to work with because they didn't respect our faith. I remember having to turn away a client after he was so disparaging and disrespectful. They had a lot of money, but it wasn't worth the investment. It was not an eternal investment.

You have to have that foundation built to be able to make a monetary decision like that.

IV – PEARL AND ARMANDO

It grew so fast it was definitely a big surprise.

Who would have thought that a real estate page based in Dallas would grow to over a million followers? We were able to make more money than we had ever made in our lives. We made enough to where we needed to spend more. It sounds crazy. But again, it is not by our work. We were used to saving money, and after selling so many homes, we had a financial advisor sit us down and advise that we spend more money. So, we went back to the prayer closet and asked God how we could be good stewards with the money He gave us. We kept coming back to the Parable of the Talents.

"14 For it will be like a man going on a journey, who called his servants[a] and entrusted to them his property. 15 To one he gave five talents,[b] to another two, to another one, to each according to his ability. Then he went away. 16 He who had received the five talents went at once and traded with them, and he made five talents more. 17 So also he who had the two talents made two talents more. 18 But he who had received the one talent went and dug in the ground and hid his master's money. 19 Now after a long time the master of those servants came and settled accounts with them. 20 And he who had received the five talents came forward, bringing five talents more, saying, 'Master, you delivered to me five talents; here, I have made five talents more.' 21 His master said to him, 'Well done, good and faithful servant.[c] You have been faithful over a little; I will set you over much. Enter into the joy of your master.' 22 And he also who had the two talents came forward, saying, 'Master, you delivered to me two talents; here, I have made two talents more.' 23 His master said to him, 'Well done, good and faithful servant. You have been faithful over a little; I will set you over much. Enter into the joy of your master.' 24 He also who had received the one talent came forward, saying, 'Master, I knew you to be a hard man, reaping where you did not sow, and gathering where you scattered no seed, 25 so I was afraid, and I went and hid your talent in the ground. Here, you have what is yours.' 26 But his master answered him, 'You wicked and slothful servant! You knew that I reap where I have not sown and gather where I scattered no seed? 27 Then you ought to have invested my money with the bankers, and at my coming I should have received what was my own with interest. 28 So take the talent from him and give it to him who has the ten talents. 29 For to everyone who has will

*more be given, and he will have an abundance. But from the one
who has not, even what he has will be taken away. 30 And cast the
worthless servant into the outer darkness. In that place there will
be weeping and gnashing of teeth."*

—MATTHEW 25:14-30

We do not want to bury our talents, so we are committed to finding new ways to invest God's money. We're not going to crawl in a corner with a pile of money.

And in the meantime, we continue to pray for families who live in the homes we sell.

V – PEARL AND ARMANDO
An invitation

When we were younger, our method of sharing the Gospel was more forceful. We preached, "hellfire and brimstone" to our friends and family who were not saved. (We probably scared some people away at first.)

Now, we see our faith as a gift and an *invitation*. It's an invitation to the best party you've ever been to! And how off-putting would it be to berate someone into attending a party? That's not an invitation, that's an *ultimatum*.

We want to introduce nonbelievers to the host of this incredible party—Jesus Christ. Now, when we evangelize, we start by telling people what Jesus Christ has done for us.

Listen up brothers and sisters. We are talking to you!

Jesus Christ took two broken people and transformed them into something whole and beautiful.

We aren't special or any different from you!

We traded a spirit of death for a spirit of life. God's love is so much deeper than anything we ever have experienced on earth.

You can choose life too!

God is our father. We were both seeking validation from other father figures whose love pales in comparison to the eternal love of God.

God is *your* father too.

God provided us with more than we could have ever imagined. And he transformed our life from the inside out.

He can transform your life too.

Our marriage would not have survived without a radical change. As our relationship with Jesus strengthened, so did our marriage.

If God can do this for us, He can do this for you.

Wives, pray for your husbands. If he is not a Christian and you are, give thanks. You have an opportunity to minister to your husband. You can show him the love you are experiencing. Remember, the Lord cares more about your husband than you! And God is calling him.

Husbands, Jesus says, "Come to me, all you who are weary and burdened, and I will give you rest." (Matthew 11:28).

It's exhausting trying to keep all the balls in the air—career, bills, family. It's overwhelming and maybe not how you pictured your life. Admit you cannot continue the way you are.

If you are ready to transform your life, let us invite you to ask Jesus into your heart right now.

The Scriptures say,

"If you confess with your mouth that Jesus is Lord and believe in your heart that God raised him from the dead, you will be savedsaved" (Romans 10:9).

You don't have to wait any longer to stop hurting.

There's no script or magical words, but here are some words to start you on your journey:

Dear Lord,

I am hurting. I have failed you and my family. I have said cruel things I cannot take back and have done things I am ashamed of. I believe you sent your son to take away these sins and sorrows. I believe you are Lord. I need you to transform my life. Please, Jesus. Save me. Please, Jesus come into my heart. Thank you, Jesus! Amen.

We are celebrating your salvation! If we don't meet you on earth, we hope to greet you in Heaven.

CHAPTER 12

How to Build
Kingdom Homes

*"Trust in the Lord with all your heart, and do not lean on
your own understanding. In all your ways acknowledge
him, and he will make straight your paths."*

—PROVERBS 3:5-6

I – ARMANDO

One of the most beautiful things we have witnessed since becoming Christians is how God has transformed our families. My father was not a believer. When we first converted, we tried to jam Scripture down his throat. He took it in stride but naturally didn't really respond to our hardline view of faith. But as we grew up in our relationship with the Lord and realized that Jesus is a God of mercy and love, we found a way to witness to him through our actions.

In 2022, our business was thriving while my Dad's business was floundering. He was in a rough spot and needed a change of pace in his career. He had lost everything he had worked for and poured himself out for other family members. He called and asked for help. He was super depressed at the time. Like me, he is motivated by working hard. I knew he needed something to get out of bed for. I also knew it was a huge phone call for him. This is the same Dad who used to pick me up in his red convertible. The same Dad who was the king of the *carne asada*. He was always bigger than life. I didn't want to see him struggle.

Pearl and I prayed about how we could not only help but also show him God's love. We could give him a one-time cash infusion, but we wanted to invest in something for eternity. We felt strongly we needed to offer him a job and bring him on board with our company.

Dad was open to the chance to work together and started handling our McAllen homes.

We taught him and my stepmother how to post videos online and do social media. I know I inherited my hustle gene from my parents because I saw a light go off in his brain, and he just went full throttle.

Let me say again, God is good.

Clients began to speak about Christ to my Dad because they knew we were a Christian company.

Over the last few years, I have seen my Dad start to really get it! He has seen the changes in Pearl and me, and he is also experiencing some radical transformation through Jesus. He's growing in Christ, so much happier, and his mood is so different.

"God is so good, Sonny, like, you know, man, son, like he's just blessing us. Like, you guys are angels, and God is so good."

And I thought, *This is my dad*? Sometimes I just stop in my tracks and praise God for making all things new.

It's been so healing for him. And for me.

Another huge change is how he loves us. He was never warm and fuzzy with us boys. And he definitely didn't say I love you. Now, this guy tells us he loves us all the time.

My dad, who was pretty darn cold and distant my whole life, is now working with me and even saying I love you! It is a miracle. All thanks to God.

I have become rich in love. I have a wife I love and who loves me—a family. And these conversations with my Dad about the Lord, man to man, have brought us all closer together. We have been making new memories together. We even did a news interview together.

II – PEARL AND ARMANDO
So, you want to start a Christian business?

It's our prayer that God continues to use our lives as a witness to Jesus's power and love.

It's by the grace of God we have been able to build the business. Whenever someone reaches out asking how to create their own Christian real estate company, we say *slow your roll*. We believe this specific business is our calling. We believe God has created us to do this job, given our personalities, family backgrounds, and strengths. We are able to settle into this gift of a calling because we know God had designed us for this. So, we have been hesitant to sell a "you can do this too," model.

We know people want to read a playbook. Follow this or do that, and you, too, can replicate success. But if you've read this book to this point, you can see we've made a lot of mistakes along the way! The success we have experienced isn't because we are amazing, it's because of God's grace and love. We want your eyes fixed on Jesus and not on us. Jesus will lead you.

What we hope to offer is simple advice based on the things we've learned over the years, and we pray the Lord fills you with his Holy Spirit and gives you a vision for your perfect calling.

So you want to start a Christian business?

1. Get in that prayer closet and open up the Word. Ask the Lord to reveal his calling for your life. Maybe it's real estate, maybe it's journalism, or being a teacher, or a full-time mom. Ask the Lord, *How can I serve your children?* Then look at what you're good at, at the gifts God has already given you. What are you really excited about?

2. Don't try to jump into someone else's calling. God has designed you for something specific. Focus on how God has called you to serve in his Kingdom and stop comparing yourself to other people. Focus on honing your craft and on being a leader in whatever role you have. You don't need to have a social media audience of 1 million to be an influencer! What has God designed YOU to do with the talents you have? Pray and ask him to reveal your strengths to you.

3. You have a ministry right now! You don't have to "start:" a Christian business. If you're a Christian, then everything you do should be your ministry. Nonbelievers are outside the church. Start where you are. Are you unemployed? Start sharing God's love with your neighbors, with your grocery clerk, with your banker, or with your social media.

4. Put on the full armor of God. Whether you are hoping to build your business online or with a hammer and nails, you're going to have to guard your heart. The internet is filled with opportunities, but it's also filled with advertisements, distractions, and chances to stumble. Make sure you put guard rails in place to protect your heart. You're entering a war zone, and you don't go into battle without training, ammunition, and gear, right? So

don't leave your house or even surf the net without guarding your heart. Temptations will come. It's important to understand your demons. You don't have to live in fear of your temptation, but you do need to know where your stumbling blocks are located. For some, it's drugs and alcohol; for others, it's food. The enemy is clever and can use anything to harm us. We can be prepared to withstand these tests by wearing the full armor of God. That is, by reading scripture daily. Surround yourself with these truths and keep praying for wisdom. You always have two voices: the voice of the Lord and the voice of the Enemy. Jesus said, "My sheep hear my voice and follow me." One of the ways to turn up the volume on God's voice is by reading scripture.

5. You're also going to need mentors and Godly leaders. You're not invincible. You're human, and you can't do this all by yourself. With my military experience, I learned that we can't lead a team without a general, right? It's better to have a general who has been through the ropes and knows what's ahead. If you're trying to do it all by yourself, and you're angry or frustrated seeing people succeed faster than you, take a step back and ask yourself who you're following.

6. Take responsibility for the actions you've made. Did you ask that woman to be your wife? Step up. Be a good husband. Live up to the vows you made. Have you hurt your spouse, or been a jerk? Own up to it. There's no shame in asking for forgiveness. But you won't be able to transform your life or your marriage if you don't allow Jesus to transform your heart and convict you of your sins. And remember, words matter. We have the power to speak life or death over our spouses, so speak with love to your beloved.

7. Don't give up on your family! Keep praying for your family. Praise God Pearl didn't give up on Armando. Praise God, we are not giving up on our family members. You are here to be a witness to your parents, siblings, cousins, and the people in your life. You don't have to travel to a remote country to be a missionary. Be a witness in your own family first and watch what happens when Jesus takes a hold of your family's life.

8. Take off the mask. Don't let yourself escape into a fantasy life, whether it's a social media personality you've created for yourself or too much time spent playing video games or watching TV. Take off the mask and look at yourself in the mirror. It's time to see yourself the way Jesus sees you. When you stop looking for the validation of man and seek the Lord's wisdom and love, you're going to be transformed!

9. God wants your whole heart. Once you accept Christ, He will work through you. The Bible is very clear about sin, right? We need to turn away from sin and repent. But you will know you're truly in Christ when you begin to grieve for your sin. His grace is sufficient. There's no need to be afraid. Jesus went to the cross to save you, not to condemn you. He's your father, and He wants your heart.

10. Stop being afraid of talking about the Lord! Your faith is not something you only practice on Sundays. If you are truly transformed in the Holy Spirit, then the Lord is always with you. Stand up for your values, and don't let people walk over you. Speak truth with boldness. Take a stand for love. People are craving that kind of authenticity.

III – ARMANDO AND PEARL
Staying in the word

Even God's gifts to us can become distractions. We believe our business is from God, but if we focus more on our brand than on our relationship with God, then suddenly everything is off-kilter. Suddenly, Armando starts to have a shorter fuse, or Pearl will begin to wallow in self-doubt.

Our entire careers have been forged with the help of social media. And our business still has a huge online presence. Social media makes you feel connected with people from around the world, but the connection with the Creator of the Universe is so much deeper.

How do we survive online?

By putting our phones and computers away. Lock them up. Get them out of your sight.

We have to have scheduled time off of social media. We will log on to do whatever work needs to be done, and then sign off for the day.

Other times we give *each other* our phones. It can be easy to spiral into insecurity if someone makes a rude comment on our videos. Or a sexualized comment may peak your interest, and suddenly you're in a conversation with a stranger halfway around the world who doesn't value your marriage. It's never been easier to throw away your vows.

When we were younger, we hid our struggles from each other because of fear, but now we are honest about our struggles. We don't fear that one argument or difficult conversation will derail our marriage because we believe the Scriptures that say, "He who began a good work in you will carry it on to completion until the day of Christ Jesus." (Philippians 1:6).God is not done with us, and He is not done with our marriage.

When we put our phones away, we dive into the scripture.

If you don't know where to begin, here's our suggestion. Start with Jesus. Start with the Book of Matthew and start to learn about the love of Jesus.

For Pearl, journaling and writing letters has helped her develop a deep relationship with the Lord.

She starts with a passage of scripture, usually only a few paragraphs. Then she writes down one verse from the passage that stirs her heart. She wants the words to stay with her, so she writes them out seven times. Afterwards, she writes a letter to the Lord to thank Him for what he's done for her and makes daily prayer requests.

We hope this helps you on your walk with the Lord if you aren't sure where to begin.

IV – ARMANDO AND PEARL
Praise God

We are relatively new Christians compared to people who were raised in the faith, and we still have a lot to learn, but one thing we want to make sure you remember is to build your foundation on solid ground. Rock solid! God is love.

Here are some other things God has put on our heart to share with you today.

- We believe things don't happen to you, things happen FOR you. Because if God is for you, who can be against you? God can use every part of your story and all of your talents.

- You are valuable because God created you, not because of what you own. Cars, jewelry, and homes are only valuable because we humans assign them value.

- Take a look around your house. From the electricity powering the lights, to the design of the couch, to the structure of the house—so much creativity went into everything the Lord has given us. And He gave us the ideas and tools to create these things.

- Change your perspective. If good things happen, praise God. If bad things happen, continue to praise God. Walk in peace and shalom.

- As God's children, we should trust Him as we would a loving parent.

- Our work is our calling. The scriptures say, "faith without works is dead."

- We set the standard high to demonstrate our faith in action. Just as a Marine in a crisp uniform embodies excellence, the bar for being a Christian should be high.

- We need to stop comparing ourselves. The grass isn't greener on the other side. The grass is greener where you water it.

- God won't bless us with more, if we don't put to use the gifts we already have now. Why ask for a bakery when you haven't even shared a loaf of bread with your neighbor?

- Maybe lust or envy isn't your jam, but what about gluttony? The scriptures say, "The wages of sin is death," and that means all sin.

- We have to stay prepared. Jesus prepared for thirty-three years before he turned water into wine for his first miracle. Consider how we often want everything immediately—our calling and our future—without putting in the necessary work.

Begin thinking about how you can be active for God. It starts at home—by praying for your spouse or family, immersing yourself in scripture, and training in prayer. It's time to become movers and builders for the Lord.

The definition of love *is* Christ. He died for you and me so that we might know His love and salvation, so that we might be transformed, so that we might become like Him. This is the good news. The gospel that saved us. The gospel that can save and transform and empower you to live confident as His beloved.

If you know God's love and can stand on His word, then, when the storm clouds come, your house will be able to withstand it, and you can change the course of the generations.

As two people who have struggled to feel loved, it's been amazing to experience our Father's love. We are His children, and we've felt so taken care of by our Heavenly Father.

From Cuba, Japan, and across the USA, the Lord has knit our stories together and made us brand new.

We have so much ahead of us. But we try to remember daily that everything is temporary. We try to keep that "eternal perspective."

Our lives are temporary. Our homes are temporary. Our bodies are temporary. We're here in this life, for a small moment, and something greater awaits us through the Lord Jesus Christ. There is an eternal home that awaits us. When we begin to have this eternal perspective, it changes the way we do business, it changes our marriages and every decision we make.

It's like we're building a house little by little. We cannot rush the process if we want a solid foundation. Today, I put another brick on the wall. Tomorrow, another brick. By the time we're thirty, forty, or fifty years old, we will have this beautiful house to pass down to the next generation.

It took us many years to undo the generational trauma and curses we inherited from our family. Praise God for breaking those chains!

"As for me and my house, we will serve the Lord."
Praise God!

Acknowledgements

To mom,

Growing up I watched you juggle the responsibilities of being a single mom and a successful entrepreneur. Watching you work tirelessly not only provided for us but also taught us invaluable skills and lessons that I carry with me to this day.

To Dad,

I've watched you work as an entrepreneur facing many setbacks along the way. Your ability to get back up is something I deeply respect. But beyond all the hard work and achievements, I am most grateful for the friendship we share.

—Love, Mandito

Para mi madre hermosa,

Gracias por darme el regalo de nunca conocer falta. Por hacer el sacrificio de dejar atrás a todos los que amaste para forjar un futuro mejor para nosotros, es un testimonio de tu coraje ilimitado y tu amor inquebrantable. Aceptaste el papel de madre y padre con gracia y fuerza. Gracias por cada sacrificio, cada momento de amor y por ser la madre extraordinaria que eres.

—Con amor, Tu Princesa

To Brandon my older brother & Cuñado,

Though you may be rough around the edges and never hold back your tongue, God has used you in profound ways to wake us from our slumber. Your honesty and forthrightness have been a blessing, shaking us when we needed it most. We admire your hard work and willingness to change.

To Marisa my Stepmother & Suegra,

You are always offering a helping hand with grace and compassion. The way you manage two daughters, a husband, and assisting with the family business is nothing short of superheroic. We want you to know it doesn't go unnoticed and are so grateful for your dedication, resilience, and selflessness.

To all our amazing clients,

Your support and encouragement have been a constant source of inspiration in our lives. You have fueled our journey with your love, grace, kindness, knowing exactly what to say when we needed it most. Many of you have become friends and family, we are eternally grateful. Thank you for being more than clients – you are cherished friends and invaluable pillars in our story.

To Our Beloved Social Media Family,

Whether you have been following since back in the early military days, the start of Nava Realty Group, or brand new to the Nava Family we thank you all. Your support has been a beacon of light in our lives. We are profoundly grateful for each one of you who has accepted us as we are and embraced our love for Jesus. Thank you for never dimming our light, for celebrating our victories, and for standing by us with your prayers during times of hardship. Your support and love have been a blessing, and we cherish every moment we've shared together.

Seven-year-old Pearl

Armando and his Dad

Armando and Pearl's
Courthouse Wedding Day

Armando during his Military days

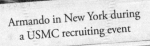

Armando in New York during
a USMC recruiting event

Armando and his Mom
& Brother at a soccer game.

Armando's first trip to Tampa
after meeting Pearl

Armando's Baptism Day

Pearl's Baptism Day

Pearl and her grandmother
on her 8th birthday.

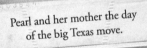

Pearl and her mother the day
of the big Texas move.

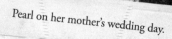

Pearl on her mother's wedding day.